To

Ashlee

From

Helen Cook

Date

_12/2018_

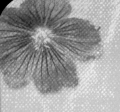

A New Beginning

God, make a fresh start in me, shape a Genesis week from the chaos of my life.
PSALM 51:10 MSG

How do you start fresh with God? How do you close the distance between yourself and your Creator? It really is very simple: Come out of hiding.

In the Bible we read the account of Adam and Eve who ate the forbidden fruit, realized they were uncovered, and hid from God. So God walked through the garden calling out, "Where are you?" God helped this couple after they stepped out into the light and said, "Here we are." Their honesty about where they were and what they had done opened the door for God to clothe them and promise them a Savior who would rescue them from their fallen condition.

God comes into our lives asking the same question: "Where are you?" When we honestly face who we are and what we have become, the door is opened for us to have a genuine relationship with Him. You can't dress up for God. He deals in the currency of honesty. Bring the real you to the real God and watch transformation take place.

Lord God, help me to admit that I...

The Habit of Making Room

Draw near to God, and he will draw near to you.
JAMES 4:8 NRSV

How do you build a relationship with God? Like a friendship or a marriage, a great relationship with God doesn't happen all at once. You build it over time. It's a daily process of investigating and celebrating who God is, and sharing the grit and substance of your life with Him.

To build a successful marriage, spouses must find time for one another, enjoying a walk in the park, a dinner at a restaurant, playing a board game, working on a remodeling project, or any of a hundred other activities. That will look different in every marriage. But, without that shared time, any marriage slowly dies.

Building a relationship with God also involves taking time out for Him. That might include singing songs of praise, silently pondering God's character, or pouring out your thoughts and feelings to Him. You might take a walk with God or invite Him to join you at work. The key isn't so much in how you approach God, but rather in the habit of making room for Him in your everyday life.

Lord, I want to make room for You today by...

....

....

....

....

....

....

....

....

....

....

....

....

JANUARY 3

Reconciliation

*When you stand praying, if you hold anything
against anyone, forgive them, so that your Father
in heaven may forgive you your sins.*
MARK 11:25

Think about how good it feels when a conflict is resolved and friendship is restored. That's what God wants for each of us.

When we iron out our differences with others and renew those friendships, we open the door for deeper intimacy with God in prayer. How do you patch things up? Follow the 1–99 rule. If the conflict is 99 percent the other person's fault and only 1 percent your responsibility, don't focus on the other party's mistakes; rather take care of your 1 percent. Most of the time, when you apologize for your role in the conflict, the other person's heart will soften.

Sincere attempts to reconcile usually work, but sometimes they don't. God doesn't expect you to take responsibility for someone else's unwillingness to apologize or forgive. Nor does God want you to invite an abusive person back into your life. But when you do your best to live at peace with all people, you will experience a new level of peace with God.

Lord God, as I take inventory of my relationships, help me to...

God's Abiding Presence

I am with you always, to the very end of the age.
MATTHEW 28:20

Where does God live? While it is true that God lives in a high and holy place as king of heaven, it is also true that God is near those who understand that they need Him. God hangs out with the humble. He spends His time with those who understand how destitute they are without Him. As a follower of God, you have the promise of His presence.

Where is God right now? He stands next to you and lives inside you. This means that He is always available. Your prayers don't need to follow some formula to reach God. They don't need to grow wings and fly into heaven. Before they leave your lips, God has heard you.

God is always listening, always attentive, always caring for and about you. This opens the door for you to share all of life with Him. You can share your thoughts, your friends, your plans, your dreams, your fears, your small talk, your deepest hurts, and your funniest jokes. Making contact with God is as simple as saying, "Here I am."

Lord God, I want to share with You today about...

_____

_____

_____

_____

_____

_____

_____

Pray Without Quitting

*The testing of your faith produces endurance; and let endurance have its full effect,
so that you may be mature and complete, lacking in nothing.*
JAMES 1:3–4 NRSV

Does it seem your prayers have gone unanswered? Never give up. Find new ways to pray, and discover new ways to see your circumstances.

This requires a combination of teachability and persistence. If your prayers are answered in a way different than you expect, ask God what He wants to teach you through the experience. Ask Him again and again to show you what you need to know. Do you need to ask for something different? Do you need to wait longer for an answer? Listen and watch for God's answers. If you are willing to learn, He is happy to teach. If you have patience, you'll find His timing is perfect. Meanwhile, keep on asking.

Persistence forges strength of character that comes from refusing to quit, even when the path isn't easy. By persisting, you join Him in His determination to make things right. Pray without quitting.

Heavenly Father, the things I want to persist in asking for are...

A Place for Prayer

He said, "My presence shall go with you, and I will give you rest."
EXODUS 33:14 NASB

The great thing about meeting with God is that you can meet with Him anywhere. He can be found on the factory floor just as readily as He can be experienced in a cathedral. If you could find a way to travel to the most distant galaxy, you would find that God is already there.

But just as a couple much in love will seek out a quiet place to be alone together, so you may also wish to find a place all your own to meet with God. You might find a place in your home where you can be free to focus on God. Or you might enjoy connecting with God outdoors along a nature trail or in a park. Maybe you would prefer to meet privately with God in a church building or mix it up so you don't get bogged down by too much routine.

As you move forward in your journey, you'll identify the atmosphere that works best for you. A place for prayer helps you grow in your friendship with God.

God, the place that works best for me to communicate with You is...

January 7

A Time for Prayer

There will be a time for every activity, a time to judge every deed.
Ecclesiastes 3:17

Prayer is a wonderful way to start your day. For a morning person, what could be better? Making prayer part of your morning routine sets the tone for your entire day. But morning isn't the only opportunity available to you. God is always available, and you can pray any time you want.

For example, you can pray several times a day at important transitions in your schedule, conversing with God during whatever natural divisions punctuate your day. You may wish to conclude your day in prayer—sharing the experiences of the last twenty-four hours with Him.

Any of these options and more are available; you can decide which best fits your personality, your lifestyle, and your season in life. By setting a time and making a plan, you move from a great idea—prayer—to a great reality—a life of prayer. Your time alone with God becomes something that you look forward to and protect. By consistently connecting with God, your soul finds the nourishment it needs and the result is a richer, fuller life.

God, for me, the best time to pray is...

Celebrating God's Presence

Do not fear, for I am with you; do not be dismayed, for I am your God.
ISAIAH 41:10

Suppose you had the opportunity to sit down with Jesus Christ in the flesh and talk with Him about anything you wanted to talk about. You could ask Him any questions, discuss any topic, share any stories, consider any plans, laugh at any jokes for as long as you wanted. What kind of time limit would you want to have imposed on that meeting?

Being free to take time to celebrate God's presence is a wonderful privilege. Some people can afford to spend an hour or longer in prayer each day. Some cannot. But praying a longer rather than a shorter time doesn't make God love you any more. God is more interested in you than He is in the clock.

He likes being with you, going to work or school with you, and joining you as you carry out your daily activities—whether that is mopping floors, planning budgets, or reading stories to children. In the sense that God is always present, we can always be praying, whether our lips are moving or not.

Lord God, this is how I feel about spending time with You...

....

....

....

....

....

....

....

Good and Great

Great are the works of the LORD, studied by all who delight in them.
PSALM 111:2 NRSV

Little children sometimes learn the dinner prayer, "God is great. God is good. Let us thank Him for our food." This simple prayer contains profound truth. God is good. He brings only good into our lives. He is never the author of any evil thing that happens to you or anyone else. But God is also great. His redemptive fingerprints are all over everything that happens to His children, so that we may emerge from tragedy and loss as victors instead of victims.

All of this becomes very personal when it comes time to trust God with the people and things you value most. As you place in God's hands what is most precious to you, you demonstrate your belief that God is good and He is great. He is good enough to want the best for you and yours, and great enough to turn every difficulty into triumph. By transferring ownership to God, you give Him an opportunity to demonstrate His faithfulness to you. You become free to be His child, resting under His care.

Heavenly Father, I have seen Your goodness when...

A Small Hop

O taste and see that the LORD is good;
happy are those who take refuge in him.
PSALM 34:8 NRSV

Blind faith has never been a requirement for following God. The so-called leap of faith is really only a small hop, like stepping across a little mud puddle, not a suicide jump across a canyon of impossibility. God allows us to verify His existence by looking into the heavens and seeing their scope and wonder, by exploring the intricate design of life and marveling at the Creator. The Bible invites us to taste and see that God is good. God wants to be experienced by you.

In a way, this journey is like courtship. As you place into God's hands more and more of the pieces of your life, you discover who God really is and how He really feels about you. You learn what He means when He says, "I love you." In your prayers, share your doubts and fears with God. Ask Him how you can discover who He really is in those areas. Let Him reveal Himself to you in a way that you can experience.

Lord God, my idea of experiencing You is...

Pray Aloud

Out of the depths I cry to you, LORD; Lord, hear my voice.
PSALM 130:1–2

There is a time and a place for silent prayer—in a library, on a bus, in school, and in many other settings where talking out loud to God might not be appropriate. But praying aloud should be part of your daily routine if at all possible. Speech helps to clarify and solidify your thoughts. A great time and place to pray aloud is when you're home, in your own room alone. But, since cell phones with Bluetooth devices have become popular, it's common to see people walking down the sidewalk in an animated conversation with someone that isn't physically present with them. You can pray aloud in public, and most people will assume you're on the phone.

Praying aloud is a great way to experience God more completely. Vocalizing your prayers also gives you practice for those situations where you might be called upon to pray for someone else. If you've never prayed with your voice before, the hardest part is getting started. Go ahead, give it a try! You'll do just fine.

Heavenly Father, when I pray aloud to You, I feel...

Affirm the Truth

The Lord is the true God, he is the living God,
and an everlasting king.
JEREMIAH 10:10 KJV

One powerful way to pray is to speak out those things you know to be true. "God, I know You are here. I know You are smarter than I am, stronger than I am, wiser than I am. My problems don't stump You at all. You're not wringing Your hands; instead, You're rolling up Your sleeves."

This is a particularly effective when you put it next to the problems you are experiencing. "I feel all alone, but I know You will never leave me nor forsake me." "I don't know what to do, but I know that You instruct me and teach me in the way I should go, that You counsel me and watch over me." "Everything is dark on my path right now, but You are the God who stood over the darkness and said, 'Let there be light.'"

These affirmations of faith strengthen your own spirit and help you keep things in perspective. Even big problems will seem small in the presence of God's great power.

Holy God, some of the things I believe to be true about You are…

The Presence of God

Blessed are those who have learned to acclaim you, who walk in the light of your presence, LORD.
PSALM 89:15

A small child was walking through a busy supermarket with her mother. All around her were bright colors and interesting shapes, sounds and smells, a whole world to explore. As her mother pondered a purchase, this child was attracted by a balloon display in the next aisle. Slipping quietly away, she went to investigate. Then something else caught her attention, and she took a few steps in that direction. This went on for a minute or two, until she looked up and realized that her mother was nowhere in sight and she had no idea how to find her. She had left her mother's comforting presence. She was lost.

The habit of prayer keeps God's comforting presence close. Life often throws things at us that we are not prepared to handle on our own.

When trouble strikes, as it usually does, without warning, you are in a much stronger place with God at your side than you would be with Him far away. Staying "prayed up" keeps you in a place of safety.

Lord, when trouble strikes, the first thing I do is...

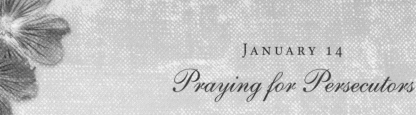

Praying for Persecutors

*I am content with weaknesses, insults, hardships,
persecutions, and calamities for the sake of Christ.*
2 CORINTHIANS 12:10 NRSV

The first mention of prayer in the New Testament is an injunction to pray for those who persecute you. Praying for those who have hurt you takes your relationship with God to an entirely different level. It affords you an opportunity to look honestly at the hurt and anger you feel, and to be realistic with God about the offenses that were committed against you. God never expects you to pretend that something bad didn't happen.

Praying for those who persecute you also allows you to examine the reasons that you might hesitate to hand that hurt and anger over to God. This is a place of honesty and truth. As you are honest with God, He can help you comprehend the freeing truth about your situation. Free from bitterness, you begin to see your persecutor through God's eyes. You can pray that he or she will come to that same place of freedom that you have found, so that everything that was wrong can finally be set right.

Lord God, when I think about those who have hurt me, I...

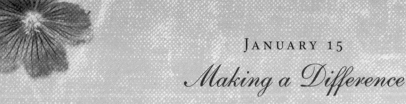

Making a Difference

Be still, and know that I am God; I will be exalted among the nations, I will be exalted in the earth.
PSALM 46:10

Your prayers for cities and nations are never wasted. You never know whose life you will change forever through prayer. The first example of intercession in the Bible is Abraham negotiating with God on behalf of the wicked cities of Sodom and Gomorrah. "If You find ten righteous people in Sodom," Abraham asks, "will You save the city from destruction?" What was Abraham thinking? Rather than focus on everything that was wrong, he looked for that sliver of hope, that opportunity for God to intervene.

In the same way, as you look around you, find opportunities for God to show up. Pray for His intervention in schools, governments, media, entertainment, families, churches, and businesses. The chaos in our world has a solution: the God who listens to and answers our prayers. The change that's needed might come through your prayers. You may never run for president or own a business or make a movie, but your influence can be felt everywhere if you are willing to intercede.

God, when I hear bad news, my first response is to...

JANUARY 16
Not a Performance

The Lord does not look at the things people look at.
People look at the outward appearance,
but the Lord looks at the heart.
1 Samuel 16:7

Many people are concerned that they don't know the right words to say when they pray. But Jesus assures us that prayer is not a performance that will be graded, but instead a moment to be shared. "Go into a hiding place and pray," Jesus says. No one needs to watch your prayers and give their seal of approval.

In a healthy family, children don't recite a script when addressing their parents; they just open their mouths and the words tumble out. In a happy marriage, spouses often speak to each other in cryptic, incomplete sentences. Their words would make little sense to someone on the outside, but, between the two of them, there's a world of meaning.

The best prayers are not necessarily the most eloquent, but rather the most heartfelt. The syntax and grammar of prayer are honesty and humility. Anyone, anytime can let go of pride and bow his or her heart before God. That posture of the heart gives all of us equal footing with God.

Heavenly Father, it's easiest for me to talk to You when...

Our Father in Heaven

I will be your Father, and you will be my sons and daughters, says the Lord Almighty.
2 CORINTHIANS 6:18 NLT

Prayer flows out of relationship. It is your connection with God that creates your conversation with God. As you come into relationship with Him, you experience Him not as some remote deity, but as your loving Father who deeply cares about you.

Earthly fathers can be awesome, aloof, abusive, or absent altogether. Your relationship with your biological or adoptive father may have been less than perfect. But things are different with Father God. He is always there for you. He understands. He always has time for you. He never forgets, never fails to keep a promise. He will encourage you and never put you down. In this relationship you can be yourself because He is here to coach you into fulfilling your true potential. When it comes time for correction, your heavenly Father always acts with kindness, never with the heavy hand of condemnation.

Knowing God's great care for you as your Father frees you to bring anything that is on your heart to Him. He will care for you.

Lord God, when I think of You as my Father, I...

Praying for Those in Authority

*Pray especially for rulers and their governments to rule
well so we can be quietly about our business of living simply.*
1 TIMOTHY 2:1 MSG

Sooner or later, people in places of power and governmental authority will make decisions, pass laws, and implement policies that you don't like. In some countries you have the freedom to enter the political process and advocate reform; in some nations you don't, but you always have the freedom to pray.

Praying for leaders is always your first and best option. Leaders are not usually available to listen to your requests, but God is. Presidents, governors, justices, and legislators sometimes make bad decisions, but God can take those poor choices and turn them around for good. God can protect you from the evil (intended and unintended) that poor leadership can bring into your life. God can give you peace and encouragement even when governments create terrible circumstances for you. Finally, God can take your prayers and use them to draw that leader into a relationship with Him.

When it comes to politics, many complain but few pray. As one who prays, you are paving the way for a better tomorrow.

God, when I think of my leaders, I most want to...

....

....

....

....

....

....

....

Anger and Prayer

I want the men everywhere to pray, lifting up holy hands without anger or disputing.
1 TIMOTHY 2:8

Can you pray when you're angry? Should you pray when you're annoyed? The answer, which may surprise you, is yes—absolutely yes. Anger is like dynamite. It can accomplish much good or it can do terrible damage depending on where and how it is used. By bringing God's presence into the heat of the moment, you can direct your anger into its most positive purpose.

Sometimes anger gives you the energy to right a wrong, to rectify an injustice, to solve a problem. But anger can also be out of propor-tion to the situation, and then prayer gives an opportunity for God's transforming presence to clear up unresolved issues.

In either case, sharing your anger first with God puts Him at the helm, where your emotions can be leveraged for the best possible outcome. "Lord, I'm angry because" is a great way to start a prayer. During the course of your conversation with God, your openness to Him will allow Him to bring wisdom for the moment, which will save a world of regret later on.

God, I find myself getting angry when...

JANUARY 20

A Shared Presence

Let us come before His presence with thanksgiving;
let us shout joyfully to Him with psalms.
For the LORD is the great God.
PSALM 95:2–3 NKJV

In courtship, a couple will probably share many different kinds of dates. Depending on their circumstances and preferences, they might go swimming together, or shopping, take a walk in a park, share a quiet meal, or go sightseeing. Some moments together will be noisy and boisterous; others will be quiet and reflective.

Your prayer journey will similarly include many different kinds of experiences with God. Sometimes you will connect with God in a noisy concert. At other times, you will share quiet moments with Him where neither of you is saying anything, but you're both aware of and appreciating each other's presence.

Prayer is not so much a collection of words as it is a shared presence. Inviting God into your world and giving Him the place of honor is at the center of prayer. What are you doing today? Invite God in. Allow Him to share life with you. Prayer "dates" can be varied and fun, just like the shared experiences of courtship.

God, today I want to invite You to join me as I...

Crying Out to God

Before they call I will answer, while they are yet speaking I will hear.
ISAIAH 65:24 NRSV

Even very young children quickly learn to call out for their parents when they're hurt or afraid. In a healthy family, a responsible dad wants to be there for his children, and a good mom will drop everything to respond to the urgent cry of a hurting child. Good parents think nothing of giving this kind of attention to their children because they understand the roles they have been given.

God's children also instinctively cry out to God in times of trouble. Self-sufficiency is great, up to a point. But all of us face troubles, dangers, and challenges that are bigger than we are. Our own resources are quickly exhausted, but God's are not.

When you're sick, in danger, confused, or hurting, go straight to God. While prayer doesn't take the place of a visit to the doctor, nor does it rule out taking prudent precautions, it brings God into your circumstances as you acknowledge that He can do what we cannot. When His children cry out to Him, He is quick to respond.

God, my biggest need right now is...

Praying for the Wayward

[God] saved us, not because of righteous things
we had done, but because of his mercy.
TITUS 3:5

As human beings created in the image of God, we were designed for perfection. But we also know that we aren't perfect, and we live in an imperfect world. In your prayers, you will intercede for those who fail, acknowledging that imperfect people need God's mercy, patience, and help.

The good news is that God loves working with ordinary, imperfect people. You can pray with confidence for those who have missed the mark, knowing that God never runs out of ideas, strategies, and tactics for helping the wayward find their way back to Him. In fact, much of God's attention is focused on reconciling flawed human beings back into relationship with Him.

As you pray for those who have failed, remember that God doesn't require people to clean up their act before coming to Him. Instead, you can be confident that God Himself will repair the damage to those who confess their inability to live up to His standard of perfection and their willingness to invite a perfect God into their imperfect world.

God, show me how to help these people to find their way back to You...

The Light of God's Presence

In him was life; and the life was the light of men.
JOHN 1:4 KJV

Visitors who tour caverns are sometimes introduced to the experience of total darkness. All the lights are extinguished as the visitors gather deep below the surface. For several moments each person strains without success to see something—anything in the pitch blackness. Then the tour guide strikes a match. The brilliance of that small flame is almost blinding.

The Bible says that God is light. He is ready to illuminate His people when they find themselves in places of darkness. Deception, hopelessness, confusion all bring shadows in our lives, but prayer punches a hole in the darkness. In the place where nothing makes sense and it seems that nothing will work, God shows up with the light of His presence. He will make a way when there is no way. In the creation account, God spoke into the darkness and created light. In the same way, He will speak into your darkest moments. When you run out of hope, direct your prayers to the God who never runs out of possibilities.

God, the place where I need the light of Your presence is...

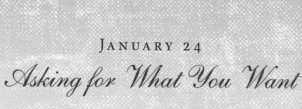

Asking for What You Want

[God] listens to the godly person who does his will.
JOHN 9:31

It's exciting to know that you, by your prayers, might shape the nature of God's intervention into human experience. Throughout the Bible, God listens to and responds to the specific prayers of His people. On one occasion, the people of God were attacked by enemy armies. Daylight was needed for a proper defense to be made and for a lasting victory to be won. The leader of God's people called out to God, asking that He delay the sunset long enough for their army to prevail. God had an unlimited number of options, but He let a human being decide which one He would employ.

In the same way, many times God simply waits to find out how you would like to proceed. He can do anything, but He sometimes gives you the role of deciding what that "anything" is going to look like.

When you pray in accordance with God's will and purpose, you often set a course of action by your prayers. Don't hesitate to figure out exactly what you want and ask God for it.

God, in accordance with Your will, I would want...

Representing God's Interests

The plans of the LORD stand firm forever, the purposes of his heart through all generations.
PSALM 33:11

As a person who prays, you represent the interests of God, looking for ways to further the purposes of God in your own life and in the lives of others. Your requests stem from your understanding of God. As you see the good that God wants to do in the lives of the people He loves, you will become bold to ask Him for what might be humanly impossible.

Your love for God will give depth and meaning to your prayers. You will gravitate toward higher motivations. For example, while you could pray for a million dollars because you want a nice house and fancy cars and luxurious vacations, your love for God might instead cause you to pray for a million dollars because you want to build and staff an orphanage in Asia. Same prayer—different motives.

Many Christians use the phrase, "in Jesus' name," when they pray. This is a way to underscore the idea that our prayer is intended to further God's good purposes on this earth. Our motive is to pray for His interests.

God, based on my understanding of what You want, here's my request...

The Perspective that Changes Everything

The fear of the Lord—that is wisdom, and to shun evil is understanding.
JOB 28:28

Understanding God's true place in the universe gives your prayers depth they would not otherwise have. As you ponder the certainty of His victory over evil, as you consider how deeply He cares, your own confidence in God's answers to your prayers will grow, and the nature of your prayers will change. You will begin to see things from an eternal perspective and long for the same things that God Himself desires.

The Bible calls this "the fear of the Lord." This is a settled determination never to go against the Almighty, a reverential awe for His majestic presence and purposes, a healthy respect for His power, and a complete trust in the goodness of His motives; an understanding that God really does know best. As you pray from this perspective, your fear of people and circumstances wanes, your faith grows, and your doubts diminish. You begin to see how God can use even a small person to make a big difference, and your prayers will echo God's deepest desires.

God, show me who You really are, especially with regard to...

A Beautiful Aroma

Let my prayer be counted as incense before you, and the lifting up of my hands as an evening sacrifice.
PSALM 141:2 NRSV

In the process of selling a home, sometimes real estate agents ask their clients to bake bread just before the house is shown to a prospective buyer. Why? Research has shown that certain smells, such as fresh-baked bread or cookies, attract buyers, while other odors, such as chlorine bleach, repel them.

Did you know that your prayers actually have a beautiful aroma? The Bible describes the prayers of God's people as "golden bowls of incense" in heaven carried by the angels into the presence of God. God loves the smell of your prayers. What you share from your heart is honored in heaven and long remembered by God.

There isn't anything you need to do to make your prayers more attractive; they already are beautiful to God because they come from an honest and sincere heart. It's eloquence of the spirit not vocabulary that matters to God. Trying to impress Him is a useless exercise. He hears and He answers because He cares deeply about you.

God, what is on my heart today is...

Preparing the Way

*Look, I am coming soon! My reward is with me, and I will give
to each person according to what they have done.*
REVELATION 22:12

Things aren't right here on planet Earth. We all know this. Sickness, poverty, injustice, and oppression are not God's intention or design. Many of our prayers will be devoted to fixing what is wrong in our bodies, our finances, our relationships, our world. The children of God continue to pray, even though many wrongs have not yet been corrected. Does it do any good? Does all this praying have any traction with God?

The Bible describes a time when God will come to earth to make all things right. What does He do first? He gathers up all the prayers of His people and pours them out on the earth. In other words, your prayers, combined with the prayers of good people throughout the ages, are preparing the way for God to fix everything that's broken in our world. Your prayers are helping to craft a new world, where everything is the way it should be. God's perfect design for humanity and creation will be restored to earth once again.

God, here's what I look forward to You fixing...

....

....

....

....

....

....

....

Intimate Friendship with God

What you're after is truth from the inside out. Enter me, then; conceive a new, true life.
PSALM 51:6 MSG

God longs to be your most intimate friend. He can be trusted with your most guarded secrets. Your prayers form the fabric of a closer and closer relationship. In your conversations with other people, discretion will guide you into being selective with what you share depending on the nature of the relationship. But those filters don't apply when it comes to your time alone with God. You truly can share anything with Him.

What are your dreams? What are your secret fears? All those things that are most personal about you are safe with God. As you invite Him into all these hidden places in your heart, you'll find yourself becoming stronger as a person because His reassuring presence will fill those places inside you that are most fragile.

Making yourself vulnerable to God actually makes you less vulnerable as a person because that spiritual intimacy becomes a source of emotional strength. Talk about anything with God and don't be afraid to go into those things that matter most to you.

God, the secret I want to share with You is...

Learning the Heart of God

Take my yoke upon you and learn from me,
for I am gentle and humble in heart.
MATTHEW 11:29

Prayer can be your opportunity to explore the heart of God. What does He care about? What is He excited about? What saddens Him? All of these are legitimate questions for you to ask when you meet with Him in prayer. While your Bible will give you a framework for understanding the heart of God, during your time of prayer and intercession you will learn how God's heart is responding to what is going on in your world.

God cares. He cries. He laughs. He cares about the things you care about, though not always for the same reasons. As you get to know God's heart, more and more you see your world through His eyes. People around you take on a new significance as fellow human beings dearly loved by God. Projects take on new meaning as you see how they fit into God's dreams and plans. Much of what was hidden before suddenly becomes clear, as you begin to feel what God feels for everything going on around you.

God, I want to understand what matters to You. Show me how You feel about...

A Change in Trajectory

This is my prayer: that your love may abound more and more in knowledge and depth of insight.
PHILIPPIANS 1:9

Prayer can lead you into life-changing moments. Your life may be set on one trajectory, but as you meet with God you may learn something that causes you to set your sights higher. God is always interested in leveraging the influence you have to bring eternal good into the lives of many, many people. But that can take different forms at different seasons in your life. Sometimes He will lead you down what appears to be a dead-end street, focusing your attention on a forgotten or marginalized person. God is orchestrating all of this because He sees possibilities and connections that you may never see.

A missionary in India once received a gift of a hundred thousand dollars. Upon earnestly praying and asking God how to use that money, he felt led by God to give most of it away to a neighbor. On the surface, it seemed ridiculous, but years later God used that gift to open the door for that missionary to reach hundreds of thousands of people.

God, I'd like to know some things about the direction I'm going, like...

Praying for Others

He performs wonders that cannot be fathomed, miracles that cannot be counted.
JOB 5:9

You never know what will happen when you pray for others. Praying aloud for others in their presence can be a powerful experience for both of you.

Your words don't need to be perfect; God knows what you mean. Consider the individuals for whom you are praying. Even if nothing changes in their circumstances, they will likely sense God's tenderness and compassion glowing through you. And they will know they aren't alone in their troubles. Your presence and your words are demonstrating that God cares, and others care as well.

Miracles happen when people pray. Maybe you've already experienced that. Money shows up at the last minute. Symptoms disappear. Addictions are broken. Marriages and other relationships are restored. Praying for others is a great way to show them you care. By inviting a great God into difficult circumstances, He can roll up His sleeves and make a difference.

Don't hesitate! Ask God for the impossible and see what He will do.

God, some people I think could use my prayer are...

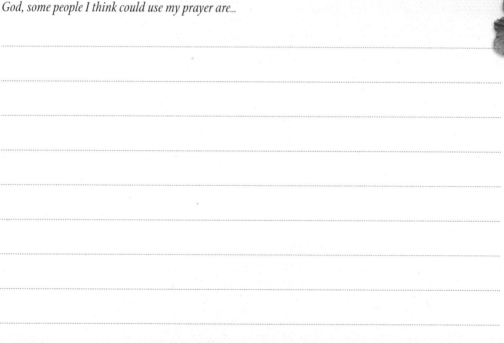

FEBRUARY 2

Unanswered Prayer

*God can do anything, you know—far more than you could
ever imagine or guess or request in your wildest dreams!
He does it not by pushing us around but by working within us.*

EPHESIANS 3:20 MSG

One of life's best teachers is a prayer that seems to go unanswered. That may seem like a strange statement, but it's true.

Sometimes these prayers mean that God wants to teach you to persevere. There may be spiritual opposition to your requests that God wants you to recognize and fight through. At other times, God may want you to make some changes in the direction you want to go. Or He may be asking you to enlarge your request. He is a big God, and He likes to do the impossible.

Even when your prayers don't seem to elicit a response, you can be sure that God has heard you, and that He's more than able to do what you've asked. So don't go away feeling slighted. Instead, investigate. Ask God to show you what is going on under the surface.

God, when I don't get the answers I expect, I will...

Learning More from Unanswered Prayer

Teach me to do your will, for you are my God. Let your good spirit lead me on a level path.
PSALM 143:10 NRSV

Prayers that don't seem to be answered are a reality for even the most devout person, the most energetic seeker of God. Even when you've prayed a prayer you feel is in everyone's best interest, you may find that an answer is not forthcoming.

When this happens, resist the urge to think your prayer is ignored. Just recognize that God does things His way and in His own timing. He always knows what's best, and He expects you to trust Him. In fact, He has been known to delay His answers at times just to see how much you've grown in trusting Him.

When your prayer seems to go unanswered, tell God you're ready to learn the lessons He wants to teach you. Open your heart and mind to discovery rather than disillusionment. Use the opportunity to gain enlightenment rather than letting disappointment color your day.

Trust God. He will never fail you. Like a good father, He will always do what's best for you. You can count on that.

God, when I don't understand, help me to...

FEBRUARY 4

Intercession by God's Spirit

The Spirit intercedes for the God's people
in accordance with the will of God.
ROMANS 8:27

While you may be limited in what you can bring to the table when it comes to prayer, there is someone right next to you who is not. God's Spirit prays with you and for you. Some requests cannot be put into words, but God's Spirit can and will articulate them clearly to God Himself.

This can be a great comfort when you don't know how to pray for a person or a situation. Simply ask the Spirit of God to make intercession for you in keeping with God's will. God's Spirit is delighted to pray for you and fill in the gaps where you cannot adequately pray on your own. He knows everything, so you can rely on His knowledge of the situation to formulate the best request. He also knows the mind and heart of God, the timing of God, the plans of God, and the desires of God. With this understanding, the Spirit can bring answers far beyond your ability to imagine.

All you have to do is ask!

Spirit of God, please pray for...

The Icebreaker

Give praise to the LORD, proclaim his name;
make known among the nations what he has done.

1 CHRONICLES 16:8

In polar regions, a special class of ships known as icebreakers move through ice-covered water, creating a path for other ships to follow. Without icebreakers, navigation in some areas would be impossible.

The discipline of giving thanks acts like an icebreaker in your soul, clearing a path for hope and joy to follow. Thanksgiving refocuses your attention on God's ultimate victory, on the good gifts He brings into your life, and on His ability to use even negative circumstances for your benefit. Thanksgiving affirms your under-standing that you are on the winning team, that loss and pain are not your final destiny, that God knows how to wipe away every tear.

As you thank God, even in the midst of distressing situations, His comforting presence draws near, and clarity about the things that really matter begins to emerge. You understand that in God you are indestructible and at His side you will prevail. You see that literally nothing can separate you from God's love, and in that love you will be and are okay.

God, I thank You for...

God's Good Plan for You

Thanks be to God! He gives us the victory through our Lord Jesus Christ.
1 CORINTHIANS 15:57

There will always be people who possess something that you don't or who have achieved something that you will never achieve. Your circumstances will never be perfect on this side of heaven. You may have even experienced great pain and sorrow. In light of these realities, how do you give thanks? Where do you start?

Begin with God's eternal plan for you, which is always good. You may be in distress at this moment, but He won't leave you there. He has heard your cry. He will come to your aid. God alone can turn the most terrible situation around for good. The darkest day in history was the day Roman soldiers nailed the Son of God to a cross. Yet God turned that into the gateway for humanity to be reconciled to Him and receive the gift of eternal life.

The same God who did that is at work in your life, turning bad situations into opportunities for good and ensuring that you end up safely in His arms.

God, thank You for the good plan You have for me, including...

The Gift of Life

Praise and glory and wisdom and thanks and honor and power
and strength be to our God for ever and ever.
REVELATION 7:12

We should all thank God for the gift of life. Our very existence comes from Him. Without Him, we wouldn't be. He designed us and put together our personalities—all the things about us that make us uniquely who we are. Even more, the Bible says that He rejoices over us and celebrates with singing.

The adventures God has for us are way too big to fit into a single lifetime, so He made us eternal beings, destined to live forever with Him. And He has given each of us the capacity to enjoy His creation with Him. He gives us brothers and sisters in the family of God to share life with.

What a wonderful benevolent God He is!

God loves you! No one can take your place in His heart. You occupy your own place in history, and you will leave a unique footprint on planet Earth. This is possible because He created you in His own image. Shouldn't you thank Him?

Wow! God, thank You for the gift of life. I am also thankful for...

....

....

....

....

....

....

....

God's Rule

*It is for freedom that Christ has set us free.
Stand firm, then, and do not let yourselves
be burdened again by a yoke of slavery.*

GALATIANS 5:1

A bad leader can be a nightmare, but a good leader is a blessing. From Herod to Hitler, history is full of examples of oppressive dictators. But leaders such as Moses and Abraham Lincoln brought people out of slavery into freedom. This is why elections are so important. Having the right person in charge matters.

Have you ever thanked God for His leadership? As you embrace His rule in your life, you move in the direction of freedom—freedom from life-controlling issues, from abusive relationships, from deception and confusion. You also look forward to the day when God's rule will extend not only to your life, but also to this earth. Everything that is wrong will be made right.

Some visions of paradise put humans at the helm, but for thousands of years humanity has demonstrated its inability to bring about utopia. As you thank God for His sovereignty, you acknowledge that only God can deliver what you deeply long for. God Himself is your solution.

God, I thank You for Your leadership when...

Security

*Let the beloved of the LORD rest secure in him,
for he shields him all day long.*
DEUTERONOMY 33:12

The famous World War II General Douglas MacArthur once said, "There is no security on this earth, only opportunity." From a human perspective, the general's commentary rings true. Even strong armies sometimes lose battles. Fortunes can be lost in a moment. Disasters can tear at the fabric of life itself. But God's Word makes it clear that security for God's people comes from a different place.

God's followers are receiving a kingdom that cannot be shaken. Real security comes only from above. God alone has the power to keep you safe in His family as His child. Jesus promises that once you are in His hand, no one can take you away.

This realization can form a foundation for your prayers. What cannot be given to you here on earth is a free gift from God in heaven. You are safe. You are secure in the Almighty. No one can touch you or tear you away from God's eternal love for you. That love will always watch over you, no matter what. In Him, you are indestructible.

God, when I think of security I imagine...

....

....

....

....

....

....

....

A Member of the Family

We always thank God for all of you and continually mention you in our prayers.
1 THESSALONIANS 1:2

When you decided to give yourself to God, He placed you in His family, and you have many brothers and sisters from all over the world and from every age and generation. Imagine how much fun it will be to listen to their stories when God gathers the family together in heaven.

Meanwhile, you can pray for the other members of God's family. The Internet and other technologies have brought the world together. Everyone is now your neighbor. Your daily prayers might include a young family in Pakistan, a journalist in Malaysia, a child in Kenya, or a retired couple in London. Their lives might look very different from your own, but you serve the same God, and under His care, you have become family.

By praying for fellow believers, you follow the example of the apostles who often began their letters to first-century churches with a summary of their prayers and thanksgiving for the people to whom they were writing. You never know how your prayers will change someone's life.

God, I pray that those in Your family will...

Building the Family

I will receive you. And will be a Father unto you,
and ye shall be my sons and daughters, saith the Lord Almighty.
2 CORINTHIANS 6:17–18 KJV

God's overall objective for humanity is to bring them—one by one—into His family. God loves people first and foremost, and they are the object of His eternal interest and care. He is not recruiting servants but adopting children, unique unpredictable individuals capable of reciprocating His love in many different ways. God's biggest sorrow is to see His love spurned by those He cares about, to see them reject His offer to include them in His family.

Your prayers can help bring people near to God who might otherwise remain far away. By advocating and interceding for those who do not yet know Him, you can have a role in the process of building up the family of God.

Lift up your prayers for those you encounter each day. Ask God to open their hearts and minds to His gifts and His goodness. In so doing, you could be gaining a spiritual brother or sister.

God, help me to pray for those who don't yet know You, like...

Mealtime Prayers

In every thing give thanks: for this is the will
of God in Christ Jesus concerning you.
1 THESSALONIANS 5:18 KJV

Mealtime prayers can be a rich opportunity to invite God into your home and into your daily routine. By welcoming the presence of God at your table, you set the stage to enjoy your meal with Him and make Him a constant companion throughout your day. And your gratitude for God's good gifts can itself be powerful.

For example, there have been reports of people facing cancer or other serious illnesses who had neither money nor insurance for medical care. These people used gratitude as their only therapy. At each meal, they fervently thanked God for the health-giving attributes of the food they were given. And they miraculously recovered.

A prayer at dinnertime can also be an opportunity to remember those throughout the world who lack food and other basic necessities and to call upon God to mobilize His people to meet these critical needs. More than anything else, pausing to acknowledge God when you sit down for breakfast, lunch, or dinner brings back perspective and helps refocus your life on Him.

God, when I connect with You at mealtimes, I feel...

Strategic Spheres of Influence

Provide people with a glimpse of good living and of the living God.
PHILIPPIANS 2:15 MSG

Have you ever stopped to think about the many different ways in which people shape human experience?

Celebrities mold popular culture and create lifestyle ideals that are followed by multitudes. Members of the media not only report on current events but shape perceptions of those events, as well. Educators build a framework for understanding and approaching all of life. Business leaders control the movement and distribution of certain resources. Elected officials, government bureaucrats, and police officers enforce policies that affect much of life. Medical professionals chart a course for health care. Religious leaders promote an understanding of God. And the list goes on.

The importance of each person's influence should not be underestimated. By remembering to pray for leaders in all of these areas, you are making a strategic decision to bring God's influence into every aspect of your life. God has a good plan for government, education, medicine, and every other area. In your prayers, you can welcome God's rule in these important spheres of influence.

God, as I think about these areas of influence, I most want...

Experiencing God's Love

Blessed be the LORD, for he has wondrously
shown his steadfast love to me.
PSALM 31:21 NRSV

You can depend on God's love. He will love you as much tomorrow as He does today, and in a thousand years that same love will still be there. The only thing that will change is your understanding and experience of that love.

In your prayers, make room for God to pour out His love. Ask Him what He wants you to know or experience. Share the scattered moments of your day with Him. Invite Him near, even when—especially when—life isn't going your way.

God's love for you is multifaceted. Sometimes He will bathe you in affirmation. At other times He will share with you the truth that sets you free from painful lies. On occasion He will gently correct you and bring you back to the path that is best for you. Each of these experiences will allow you to "taste and see that God is good." Amidst the storms of life, His love will strengthen you and give you peace.

God, I want to hear what You have to share with me today because...

The Discipline of Prayer

Discipline isn't much fun. It always feels like it's going against the grain.
Later, of course, it pays off handsomely, for it's the well-trained
who find themselves mature in their relationship with God.
HEBREWS 12:11 MSG

Prayer can be a delight. But what about those times when it isn't? All of us have times when we feel like our prayers are bouncing off the walls and going nowhere. Here's where you can take your cue from world-class athletes, musicians, and other performers.

These highly successful individuals never stop practicing even when it's boring, even when they would rather be doing something else. In fact, only those who spend thousands of hours in practice reach that world-class status. To be their best, they have to practice whether they feel like it or not.

Similarly, everybody has days when they would rather be doing something instead of praying. Getting to the best that God has to offer you in prayer means persevering through the everyday discipline of praying, even when you'd rather be watching television, shopping, or playing volleyball. There's room in life for all these other activities, but if you keep prayer as a priority, the rewards will amaze you.

God, empower me to be faithful in prayer, especially when...

Praying for Open Eyes

I do not cease to...remember you in my prayers...that,
with the eyes of your heart enlightened,
you may know what is the hope
to which he has called you.
EPHESIANS 1:16, 18 NRSV

When the apostle Paul prayed for others, he asked that their eyes would be opened so they could see who God really is and how much He loves and cares for them. You can do the same. In fact, some people take Paul's words from the Bible and actually pray those words for the people they love. You can do that or simply take the concepts and incorporate them into how you formulate your prayers.

The apostle understood that your concept of God governs everything in your life. It's not so much the theology you believe, as it is your gut-level, deep-seated beliefs about God. Do you know that God is good? Do you trust Him even when disaster strikes? Do you know that He loves you even when circumstances say otherwise? Are you confident that He keeps His promises? As you pray for others, ask God to give them this settled knowledge of Himself. With that understanding, they can weather any storm.

God, open people's eyes to see...

Praying for Enemies

Do not repay evil with evil or insult with insult.
On the contrary, repay evil with blessing, because to this
you were called so that you may inherit a blessing.
1 PETER 3:9

In the Gospels, Christ commands us to love our enemies and pray for those who persecute us. How do you do that? It begins with an understanding of where the real battle is taking place. When human beings become the agents of evil, they arrive in that place because they are trapped in a web of deception. While they may be perpetrators of harm, they are also victims of evil. They need the same experience with God that you have. You can pray that they will discover that God is good.

Sometimes, of course, our enemies are not terrible people at all, but instead people who rub us the wrong way, people whose personalities clash with our own. In this case, your prayers for that person will begin to build a bridge of understanding between the two of you. Deep down inside, almost everybody has the same needs and desires. By finding out what you have in common, you may end up gaining a friend.

God, I pray that my enemies would...

Fasting and Prayer

Is not this the kind of fasting I have chosen: to loose the chains
of injustice and untie the cords of the yoke,
to set the oppressed free and break every yoke?
ISAIAH 58:6

When Jesus began His ministry, He spent forty days in fasting and prayer. Throughout the ages, men and women of God have combined fasting and prayer as a way to purify their hearts and focus their energies on God and His purposes. Fasting has a way of clarifying what's important in your life.

People fast in many ways: skipping a meal, going a day or longer without food (but not without water), abstaining from dessert for a week, forgoing television for a month, and so on.

The specifics are between you and God, though people with medical conditions should consult their physician before embarking on a fast.

Many people experience powerful spiritual growth during these seasons of self-denial. Temptations may peak during or just after a fast (as they did for Jesus), but afterward you may experience a much greater ability to resist the urge to do wrong. If your prayers are unanswered, fasting may provide the breakthrough you need.

God, this is what I understand about fasting...

....

....

....

....

....

....

Planting Possibilities

*Jesus said, "Let the little children come to Me,
and do not forbid them; for of such
is the kingdom of heaven."*
MATTHEW 19:14 NKJV

An important part of Jesus' ministry was welcoming, blessing, and praying for children. None of those prayers are preserved in the Bible, so we can only imagine what He may have said. But He did set a precedent for us to pray for the children in our lives.

Inviting God to intervene in the life of a child is an act of hope. You are planting the seeds for a better tomorrow. God has a rich interest in the lives of these little ones. It's no accident that most people form a relationship with God early in life. Even as you're out walking or driving, you can breathe a silent prayer for the children you pass. You never know what God might do with those prayers.

In the early 1800s, Johnny Appleseed scattered seeds throughout the midwestern United States. The result was hundreds of thousands of apple trees. In the same way, through your prayers you can plant new possibilities in the lives of children wherever you go.

God, some of the children I would like to pray for are...

Inviting Others In

Carry each other's burdens, and in this way you will fulfill the law of Christ.
GALATIANS 6:2

Don't hesitate to ask others to pray with you and for you. On several occasions in the Bible, kings and other leaders asked people to pray for them. This was always understood as a sign of prudence, never as a sign of weakness. Even Jesus asked His disciples to join Him in prayer.

When you invite others into your circle of prayer, you give them an opportunity to share ownership of whatever answer God provides. You also affirm the value of their contribution.

Many will be honored to pray with you. Some will be reluctant to pray out loud in your presence, but their prayers in silence or in secret matter just as much. Different people will have different styles and will relate to God in a variety of ways. Their style might not be yours, but there is always strength in diversity. Others often approach the same situation with a totally different and helpful angle.

Open your heart and prepare to receive a new perspective on your situation.

God, the people I'd like to ask to pray for me are...

Prayer and Music

Serve the LORD with gladness; Come before His presence with singing.
Know that the LORD, He is God.
PSALM 100:2–3 NKJV

When confronted with the need to hear from God to resolve a wartime crisis, a prophet made an interesting request: "Bring me a harpist," he said. He wanted music. For him, that was the fastest way to get into the presence of God. Music can be a powerful gateway into prayer. It can quiet and focus your thoughts or send your heart soaring in praise.

What kind of music? That will vary by individual and with the moment in time. Many people wouldn't think of praying without turning on a praise album. Others prefer quiet piano or other instrumentals, or even Gregorian chants. Others will connect with God through rock, jazz, rap, hip-hop, or some other style. You might prefer to listen, or you might sing along. And dancing before the Lord is a time-honored tradition.

If you're praying and you get stuck, sometimes a CD or iPod player is exactly what you need to get things moving again. Harness the spiritual quality of music and use it to go deeper in your relationship with God.

God, I think music inspires prayer because...

A Prayer Notebook

Guard my teachings as the apple of your eye.
Bind them on your fingers; write them on the tablet of your heart.
PROVERBS 7:2–3

Are you keeping a prayer log? Writing down your requests, your answers to prayer, and what you feel God is saying to you can be very helpful. It can be as simple or as elegant as you like, but keeping some kind of record can be encouraging and instructive for many reasons. When you go through seasons of doubt and discouragement, your own record of answered prayers will build and strengthen your faith. You might also want to share your story of answered prayers with those who are exploring a relationship with God.

A prayer log is also helpful as you seek to understand what God might be saying to you. If you see certain themes repeated again and again over time, this is more likely to have come from God than just a random thought that may have popped into your head. These themes can be discussed with a pastor or other spiritual mentor who can help you nail down the substance of what God may be sharing with you.

God, thanks for answering my prayer about...

FEBRUARY 23

Getting Results

LORD, I wait for you; you will answer, Lord my God.
PSALM 38:15

Your prayers have just as much value as those of anyone else. It may be tempting to think you need some sort of "prayer celebrity" to pray over you or for you in order for your prayers to be answered. But God listens to the prayers of all His children.

While it is true that some people have more gifting, experience, and training in prayer, anyone can pray earnestly and see God answer. Throughout the Bible, we see examples of ordinary people praying for God's intervention and getting answers to their prayers.

What was their secret? Two things: First, they really wanted what God wanted. They prayed according to His will. They enthusiastically guarded His reputation. They wanted God's purposes to come out ahead. Second, they took the time to ask and keep on asking for what they wanted. They didn't give up. Their persistence, coupled with their desire, made the difference. Their prayers were answered.

You can follow their example and see the same results.

God, help me to desire what You want in regard to...

Prayer and Healing

*Are any among you sick? They should call for the elders
of the church and have them pray over them,
anointing them with oil in the name of the Lord.*
JAMES 5:14 NRSV

Research done by secular medical professionals is only now discovering the role prayer plays in health care. But the Bible has always told of its benefits. For example, in the New Testament, believers are instructed to call on the leaders of their church to pray for them when sick.

Prayer serves as a reminder that health and healing come from God. As you pray for others and they pray for you, health-sustaining community is formed and a healthy bond of interdependence is forged. Prayer helps the afflicted to focus their mental energies on recovery. Prayer invites a supernatural God to do what only He can do.

Sometimes God will grant instant recovery in response to your prayers. Sometimes your intercession will assist medical professionals as they do their work. In most cases, your prayers for the suffering will comfort them and remind them that there are people in their lives who care.

God, for those around me who are suffering, I ask You to...

Extending Your Influence

Hear a just cause, O Lord; attend to my cry; give ear to my prayer from lips free of deceit.
PSALM 17:1 NRSV

You may never have the opportunity to visit a prison camp in North Korea, an orphanage in Uganda, the Oval Office in Washington, a refugee camp in Sudan, or guerrilla headquarters in Colombia. But your prayers can go to all of those places and more. As you plead with God on behalf of those who are suffering, those who need direction, those who need provision, your influence enters places and arenas that you never could. You will leave a worldwide footprint because you cared enough to pray.

Right now the influence you have is hidden. You may never hear reports back from the many people you are praying for all over the world. But someday everything will be revealed. In heaven, you will meet people who have received eternal benefit from your intercession on their behalf. You might not know their names right now or much about their circumstances, but someday they will be your friends, your brothers and sisters for eternity.

God, as I pray for those I don't know, show me...

Praying for Those in Prison

Remember those in prison as if you were together with them in prison,
and those who are mistreated as if you yourselves were suffering.
HEBREWS 13:3

Did you know that much of the New Testament of the Bible was written by someone in prison? Throughout the ages and even in the present, God's people have often been imprisoned because of their faith. In addition, many incarcerated criminals have found God during the course of their prison experience.

In your prayers, remember those in prison. While most people want to forget those who are behind bars, God does not forget them. God is still at work in their lives and still cares deeply about them. You can pray that prisoners and prison officials experience God in a life-transforming way. You can pray that God's followers are given strength to lead others into a relationship with Him. You can pray that those who have been falsely imprisoned would quickly be restored to their families and friends.

Prison need not be a dead end street. Instead, it can be an incubator for life-changing miracles.

God, when I think of those in prison, I ask You for...

The Battle in the Mind

You will keep him in perfect peace, whose mind is stayed on You, because he trusts in You.
ISAIAH 26:3 NKJV

War and the threat of war has been a human reality for thousands of years. But beneath the surface, the real battle is in the mind. Most of mankind's problems flow from faulty thinking. If each person on earth deeply understood, appreciated, and experienced God and His love, many of the problems that plague humanity could be quickly resolved. Global poverty could be eradicated. Hunger would be wiped out. Oppression and injustice would no longer occur. Wars would end.

As you pray for others, keep in mind that you are interceding for their minds. You are asking for an open door so that they can voluntarily welcome God into the center of their experience and discover in Him the truth that sets them free. While God will not force Himself on anyone, you can pray that the layers of deception will be removed so that others can make clear decisions in favor of God and begin to experience Him on a deep life-changing level.

Miracles first take place in the mind.

God, please work in the hearts and minds of...

Wrestling in Prayer

Let us hold fast the confession of our hope without wavering,
for He who promised is faithful.
HEBREWS 10:23 NKJV

The Bible speaks of "wrestling in prayer." Why would you need to fight if you are having a conversation with your loving Father in heaven? Wrestling in prayer acknowledges two realities: First, you will encounter spiritual opposition to your prayers. The more you want what God wants, the more the forces of evil will oppose you. Second, sacrifice strengthens commitment. Within reason, the more you wrestle, the greater your determination will be to pray for what you want.

How do you wrestle? Keep coming back to God for wisdom. Rejoice in God's purposes and timing. Determine to want what God wants. Speak out what you want. Pray against opposition. Refuse to get discouraged. Never give up.

Some things are worth fighting for, like the eternal destinies of those you love, God's reputation here on earth, the well-being of God's followers around the world. By wrestling in prayer for the things that matter, you will make a profound difference in many lives. Your tenacity can lift others out of desperate situations and restore hope for them once again.

God, I want to learn to wrestle in prayer. Teach me to...

Praise-Filled Prayers

*Praise and exalt and glorify
the King of heaven, because everything
he does is right and all his ways are just.*
DANIEL 4:37

Bible school professors routinely teach their students to praise God before bringing their petitions to Him, and then to follow those petitions with more praise and thanksgiving. Why would this be important? Is God some kind of egomaniac who needs to be buttered up before He is willing to help us?

Of course, God delights to hear that His children love and appreciate Him—what father doesn't? But God doesn't necessarily need our praise. He is benevolent by nature. He wants to answer our prayers. He wants to pour out His blessings on us.

Filling your prayers with praise to God for who He is and what He's done is for your good. It serves as a reminder of God's faithfulness. He has never failed you and He won't fail you now. Praising Him also reminds you that God is great and powerful and more than able to grant the requests you are placing before Him.

Make praise the greatest part of your prayers. Your faith will be greatly strengthened.

Lord, I want to praise You for...

A Difference You Can Make

I have said this to you, so that in me you may have peace.
In the world you face persecution.
But take courage; I have conquered the world!
JOHN 16:33 NRSV

Are you uplifted by the stories of people who have overcome overwhelming odds? As a person of prayer, you can become part of someone's inspiring story, particularly when you pray for those who are persecuted for their faith. In many nations it is dangerous or illegal to follow Christ. As you reach out to these followers of God through your prayers, you join them in their struggle and own a piece of their ultimate triumph.

How can you help? As you remember them in your prayers, you can ask God to strengthen them and give them wisdom. You can ask for families to be restored and for justice to take place. You can pray against mob violence and inhumane treatment. Most of all, you can pray that your brothers and sisters will persevere in their faith and help others around them know the same hope that you have discovered.

People you have never met will feel your prayers and will be greatly encouraged by them.

God, my prayer for those who are persecuted is...

A Person of Influence

[God] does not ignore the cry of the afflicted.
PSALM 9:12

Maybe you've seen God answer prayer in your own life and the lives of your loved ones, but have you ever stopped to realize how much good your prayers can do for the world in general? Like most people, you may feel you have little muscle in this world, but your prayers can mean the difference between life and death.

Your prayers can affect decisions made by government leaders, corporate CEOs, and church administrators. The possibilities are endless. But have you ever imagined that your prayers can also affect the decisions of despots and dictators? Your petitions to God could save the life of a missionary serving in a foreign land or innocent children born under the rule of a corrupt regime.

God has called each of us to do great and powerful things through prayer. That includes protecting the innocent and bringing evil governments down to the ground. It's possible, even probable, that nothing else you do will make such a powerful difference in this world.

God, us my prayers to influence...

Praising God

From the throne came a voice saying,
"Praise our God, all you his servants,
and all who fear him, small and great."
REVELATION 19:5 NRSV

Do the everyday annoyances of life ever seem to gang up on you? When troubles seem overwhelming, it's a great time to pull out the prayer warrior's secret weapon: praise. As you focus on God's goodness and greatness, everything seems to fall into place. Even larger problems become more manageable as you remember the goodness of the God who holds your life in His hands. Praise paves the way to trust, which opens the door to intimacy in your relationship with Him.

When facing health challenges, you can praise the God who will someday cause you to walk in perfect health forever. If financial woes strike, fight back by praising God as your provider, your mentor, your coach, the One who gives you the ability to produce and manage wealth.

In the famous story of David and Goliath, David's victory was made possible because he was in the habit of lining God up next to his problems and discovering that God was a whole lot bigger.

God, I praise You for my...

Greater Than His Gifts

*In everything you do, put God first, and he will
direct you and crown your efforts with success.*
PROVERBS 3:6 TLB

As you think through God's many gifts, do you ever stop to ask which is the greatest of all? Would it be the health God provides? Or would His greatest gift be family, friends, and relationships? Then again, the peace and joy, opportunities and strength God grants are all priceless. But there is a gift that rises to the top and towers over everything else that God can give. That gift is God Himself. The greatest answer to prayer is not healing or a miracle or a million dollars. The greatest answer to prayer is God Himself because God is greater than His gifts.

By seeking God first in your prayers, you invite Him to journey through life with you, even if you never get healed or get out of debt or get that perfect marriage or family that you desire. For the man or woman who is patient in prayer, God shows up and all His other gifts eventually follow. The presence of the Giver gives every other gift its value.

God, I value You over Your gifts because...

If Feelings Could Talk

Let the words of my mouth and the meditation of my heart be acceptable in Your sight, O Lord.
PSALM 19:14 NKJV

Suppose you could find a lonely spot on a deserted beach to have a long and intimate conversation with God. Nothing is off limits; you can talk about anything. What would you discuss? If you're like most people, you would probably let Him know what's going on in your heart and share the feelings you are experiencing.

As you think about the feelings you might share with God, one way to frame the conversation might be to answer the question, "If my feelings could talk, what would they say?" The answer might not make logical sense, but it will make "feeling" sense—and that is worth sharing with God. Because feelings reflect your inner self, this is a great way for you to invite God to share Himself with you.

Sometimes a simple whisper from God's Spirit can completely reorient your feelings. It can be like throwing open the blinds to let the sun shine in. Sharing your feelings with God creates an opportunity for Him to pour out His love on you.

Heavenly Father, if my feelings could talk, they would say...

Spiritual Muscle

Do what is right and true.
Be kind and merciful to each other.
ZECHARIAH 7:9 NCV

Every spring, you find farmers out in their fields preparing the ground and planting seeds. Have you ever thought about how your acts of kindness are like seeds that could some day bring in a harvest? Whether you write a note of encouragement to a friend or stop by the home of an elderly person to repair an appliance or shield a child from a school bully, you will have countless opportunities to do good over the course of your lifetime.

Just as the seeds planted by a farmer need to be watered in order to grow, as you do generous acts, you can help them grow in their impact on others by bathing your efforts in prayer. This creates a partnership between you and God, where He can weave together circumstances and connections to take your simple act and give it far-reaching results. As you water your deeds with prayer, God will oversee the results and use your good works to bring eternal benefit into many, many lives.

God, show me how to use my spiritual muscle for...

A Letter to God

Write this down, for these words are trustworthy and true.
REVELATION 21:5

Have you ever written and hand-delivered a letter to a close friend or family member? Even though you could easily talk to this person face-to-face or over the phone, perhaps you found it easier to gather your thoughts and articulate your feelings through the written word. Because you may express yourself better or differently when you write, writing a letter to God offers you the opportunity to share another part of yourself with Him.

Writing forces you to focus and clarify your thoughts, so writing a letter can be a good tactic when you aren't quite sure how you feel about a certain issue. It also provides you with a record of your prayers, so you can look back and see what God has done in response to them.

Whether you compose elegant prayers on formal stationery or scribble notes on scrap paper or pound away on a keyboard, writing a letter to God can be a method by which you connect with God in a deeply creative and intimate way.

Dear God, my letter to You would begin...

Write It Out

[Jesus said], Everything is possible for one who believes.
MARK 9:23

What are your most important beliefs? Your core beliefs should correspond closely to those truths that have stood the test of time such as those expressed in the Bible. Writing out these beliefs and reading them aloud in your time of prayer can be a powerful faith-building exercise.

You may want to write something like, "I am a success because God's work in me will not fail," or "I will love because God first loved me." Throughout history, many people have written out "confessions" such as these. Among the most famous are the *Confessions* of St. Augustine. For example, he wrote, "Our hearts are restless until they find rest in You [God]."

As you write out what you know and believe to be true about God, about life, about yourself, your own faith becomes more focused and clarified. Reviewing these statements can encourage you and those around you to do more and be more. Read them regularly in your prayer time and meditate on them. Your beliefs more than any other thing help you define who you truly are.

God, some of the things I believe to be true are...

Steady Thoughts

Commit thy works unto the LORD, and thy thoughts shall be established.
PROVERBS 16:3 KJV

Do you ever have trouble focusing your thoughts when it comes time to pray? Prayer can be enormously rewarding, but at times it can be hard work. If your mind is all over the map when you just want to have a conversation with God, there are many things you can do to help focus your attention. One possibility is to audio record the part of your prayer that you come back to day after day. This might be a statement of your key beliefs, a list of things that you like about God, key requests, or a recitation of the things you are most grateful for in this season of your life.

Recording and replaying these things can help you get started with your prayer each day. This is particularly true if you are an auditory thinker. This is one of many creative ideas you can use to get yourself in the right frame of mind when it comes time to give God your full attention.

God, here is what I want to come back to every day...

....

....

....

....

....

....

....

Praying the Psalms

*Let everything that breathes sing praises
to the LORD! Praise the LORD!*
PSALM 150:6 NLT

Imagine what it would be like if your brothers hated you, your employer tried to kill you, your spouse was taken away from you, and your sons rebelled against you and meant to do you harm. This was the life of King David. Yet despite all the trouble he experienced, he always landed on both feet, with his eyes heavenward, believing with all his heart in the goodness of God.

David kept a journal of his prayers during those tumultuous years. Those prayers were later turned into songs and recorded in the Bible in the book of Psalms. Because many of these prayers were written during times of distress, they capture deep human longings, and can sometimes express feelings that you might not be able to put into words. The Psalms also contain soaring expressions of praise that will inspire you to know God intimately.

Opening the Psalms, reading them aloud, and praying through them can greatly enrich your time alone with God and reassure your heart that the great God who reigns in heaven is watching over you.

God, the Psalm that speaks most to my soul is...

....

....

....

....

....

....

....

....

Discovering God

All Scripture is inspired by God and is useful to teach us what is true.
2 TIMOTHY 3:16 NLT

What would it be like if you could step through a door and on the other side, discover amazing secrets about God, some of which are thousands of years old? How would that impact your time alone with God? In actual fact, you can learn those secrets, not by opening a door but by opening the Bible. Many people make studying the Scriptures their life's work because the Bible is a well of information and inspiration that never runs dry.

Combining Bible reading and prayer is an age-old tradition that yields all kinds of benefits. It builds your faith. It connects you with thousands of years of history, and it empowers you to better understand God's perspective on everything from marriage to politics.

As you pray through the things you read, not only do your prayers gain greater focus, but you become better able to discern which of your thoughts and feelings originate from the mind and heart of God and which do not. Your understanding of the Bible and your intimacy with God will grow.

God, as I read the Bible I find myself thinking...

_____

_____

_____

_____

_____

_____

_____

Let's Ask Together

Again, truly I tell you that if two of you on earth agree about anything
they ask for, it will be done for them by my Father in heaven.
MATTHEW 18:19

Being alone in conversation with God is a wonderful thing. But the Bible tells us that praying with others has even more benefits.

Joining your prayers with others deepens the bond of intimacy between those involved. Conflicts are settled and laid aside and all feel the strength and encouragement that comes from a shared commitment to something important. Jesus told His disciples that our prayers are especially powerful when they are shared.

Think of it this way. Remember when you were a child and you and your siblings or your friends went together to your parents to make a request? Your parents were more inclined to listen to all of you than just one of you. Right?

So come together and lift your voices together. Share your individual insights and understanding and then find a comfortable level of agreement and make your request known to God.

Heavenly Father, the people I would like to agree with are...

_____

_____

_____

_____

_____

_____

_____

A Double Blessing

We have not stopped praying for you. We continually ask God to fill you with the knowledge of his will through all the wisdom and understanding that the Spirit gives.

COLOSSIANS 1:9

A brief prayer can be a powerful tool for imparting confidence and wisdom to others, especially those who look to you for guidance. In the Bible, we read that King David came home to bless his family. You too can bless your family by praying for them in their presence.

For example, you might pray, "Thank You for my daughter's beautiful spirit. Let her know that she is treasured and loved. Give her wisdom in all she does today. Let her be an encouragement to everyone she meets." While prayers are not, of course, a good forum for correction or preaching, they can be powerfully used to build up those you love. You might even put a hand on a person's shoulder to convey your love if it is appropriate for the relationship. If you do it in a respectful manner, this is a great way to build up those you love most.

There is something very special about praying for those you love. It blesses everyone involved.

God, those I would like to bless are...

....

....

....

....

....

....

....

Keeping You in Sight

See, I have engraved you on the palms of my hands;
your walls are ever before me.
ISAIAH 49:16

Maybe you've experienced the satisfaction of taking someone's hand, praying for that person, and seeing God intervene in his or her life. As wonderful as that is when it happens, sometimes it's not practical to be in the presence of the person for whom you are praying. But there are ways to keep that spiritual and emotional connection.

Some people find it helpful to pray over a photograph of the person for whom they are interceding. This helps to ignite their imagination and allows them to focus with greater clarity as they pray. Whether the image is a sponsored child in Asia or an aunt in Cincinnati, you can sometimes see needs in a photographed face that words cannot express.

Whether you put up photos as prayer reminders on your refrigerator, organize images in an online collection, or include portraits in a prayer notebook, photos can take a family member that you see every day or a child halfway around the world that you may never meet, and bring them near as you lift them up in prayer to God.

God, as I look at these photos, I pray...

....

....

....

....

....

....

....

Which Way to Pray

O come, let us worship and bow down, let us kneel before the Lord, our Maker!
PSALM 95:6 NRSV

What would you expect to find if you did an online image search for "prayer"? If you imagined folded hands, bowed heads, and closed eyes, you have a good idea of how prayer is normally pictured. And that prayer posture works great for many people, reminding them that God is higher than we are, that He is worthy of our respect, and that it is worth it to close out all distractions and focus solely on Him.

But have you thought about other ways to pray? One man complained that every time he prayed over his lunch at work, his coworkers stole his meal from him. He asked God what he should do, and got this response: "Pray with your eyes open." Some people like to pace when they pray. It allows them to pour more energy into their prayers. Some pray best when sitting or lying on the floor.

It never hurts to try something new. A different posture might make a difference for you, or it may help you express a different side of yourself to God.

God, when I pray, I like to...

God's Kingdom for Your Life

The kingdom of God is not a matter
of eating and drinking, but of righteousness,
peace and joy in the Holy Spirit.
ROMANS 14:17

Of all the possible lives you could live from this point forward, which one would be best? Which one will you look back on and be happiest with? Prayer can be the bridge that takes you from where you are now to the life you truly want. When you pray for God's leadership in your life, you're really asking for the best possible life. Jesus had a way of describing this. He instructed His disciples to ask that God's kingdom would come.

What was He getting at? A kingdom with the right king brings order and peace, safety and prosperity to a nation. In the same way, God's leadership in your life brings personal peace, wisdom, and direction. God is not a bully; nor is He a micromanager. You don't cease to be the unique person you are, but rather you are empowered to be all God created you to be. Your dreams are purified, validated, elevated, and made possible by God's presence and rule. Putting God in charge ultimately makes everything okay.

God, please bring Your kingdom to my life. Help me to...

God's Kingdom for Your World

All of your works will thank you, Lord, and your faithful followers will praise you.
They will speak of the glory of your kingdom; they will give examples of your power.
PSALM 145:10–11 NLT

Suppose you could unlock the door to a better life for the people you know and love. What would give you the power to do that? Your connection with God. As you pray for God's kingdom to arrive, you are asking for a whole new dimension of living for the people in your world. God is able to do far above and beyond all that you can ask or imagine. His plan always involves empowering people to reach their highest potential. His plan always shelters the needy and the fragile and gives them the power to live life with dignity and purpose.

While your prayers can't make other people's choices for them, your intercession can help bring good choices into focus. God's plans are good; His presence is transforming. Your prayers invite both. As you welcome God's rule into your church, your community, your region, your nation, your world, who knows how great the impact might be!

God, when I think about Your kingdom coming to my world, I...

Forgiving Others

Be ye kind one to another, tenderhearted, forgiving one another,
even as God for Christ's sake hath forgiven you.
EPHESIANS 4:32 KJV

It's difficult to imagine anyone who has been wronged, betrayed, or abused, and who has not struggled to forgive. We've all been there. And the worst part is that the greatest offenses often take place in our closest relationships.

It's refreshing to know that God doesn't expect us to ignore or minimize these wrongs. On the contrary, He invites us to look at them honestly, to know and feel the anger and hurt He feels that we are treated poorly. But then He invites us to a better place where those hurts no longer have any power in our lives. He asks us to forgive. This may sound impossible, and apart from God, it is. But God holds out His hands to receive our anger so we don't need to carry it anymore.

Right now, God is ready to help you cancel the offender's debt. Reach out in prayer on behalf of the person who has offended you. Release your hurt to God and be set free.

God, the person I most need to forgive is...

Eager to Forgive

*If we confess our sins, he is faithful and just
to forgive us our sins, and to cleanse
us from all unrighteousness.*
1 JOHN 1:9 KJV

Wouldn't life be a whole lot easier if we were all perfect? No one would ever need to apologize, and we wouldn't need to be concerned about breaking God's standard of behavior for our lives. Unfortunately, none of us is perfect; sooner or later we all make a wrong choice—we say an unkind word, think harmful thoughts, or cross the line in some other way—and find ourselves in need of God's forgiveness.

It may seem hard to walk into God's presence with that fault in hand and the need to admit an error, but here is where you will find God to be most approachable. He rushes to forgive those who freely admit their helplessness to please Him apart from His empowering grace. He is happy to cleanse you from whatever caused you to go down the wrong path, and to work with you to tame those desires that may continue to pull you in a self-destructive direction.

Forgiveness comes from God, and He is eager to restore you when your heart is humble before Him.

God, the things I need to confess to You are...

Asking for What You Want

If we ask anything according to his will, he hears us.
And if we know that he hears us in whatever we ask,
we know that we have obtained the requests made of him.
1 JOHN 5:14–15 NRSV

Have you ever made a list of the things you want? From hula hoops to husbands, from Corvettes to college degrees, our list of needs, wants, and desires creates great opportunities for prayer. Because prayer is a partnership between you and God, God wants you to tell Him what you want. He wants you to ask. In return, He promises to satisfy your desires with good things. While, of course, He doesn't give everything everybody asks for at the moment when they ask, in the long run, He grants requests or provides something even better. Your part is to ask and keep on asking.

In the process of asking, your prayers become teachable moments where God inspires you to dig deeper and reach for something higher than you ever imagined asking for before. Yes, your prayers will be answered. But as you and God engage in conversation around these needs, you will receive far more than you even knew how to request.

God, here is what I want...

Avoiding Temptation

Watch and pray so that you will not fall into temptation.
The spirit is willing, but the flesh is weak.
MATTHEW 26:41

Sometimes it may seem like the harder you try to follow God, the harder it becomes to do so. There is a simple explanation for that: The influence of evil is never far away. Doubt, fear, lust, greed—all of us experience temptations like these and more. But this is where prayer makes a big difference. By asking God to keep you away from those allurements that could entice you down a self-destructive path, you can avoid many of those side streets.

Your prayer might sound something like this: "God, please mark out a path for me today and command temptation to stay off it." If ungodly enticements are a challenge for you, you may be surprised at how powerful a simple prayer like this can be. When you don't need to struggle all day with the lure to do wrong, it's amazing how much energy is freed up to do the things you want to do. It's called being proactive in prayer.

God, the temptation I am most vulnerable to is...

Deliverance from Evil

He who keeps you will not slumber....
The LORD shall preserve you from all evil.
PSALM 121:3, 7 NKJV

Do you ever feel like you are in a battle? Sometimes, the more you seek to follow God, the more the forces of evil will seek to oppose you. But here's the good news: You have a bodyguard: God Himself. As you remember to ask God to deliver you from evil, you bring into focus the reality that you are in a battle, but you are on the winning side. The Bible says that our real enemy is not flesh and blood but spiritual forces of evil.

Because many people do not clearly understand the role of good and evil in their lives, they fall prey to traps that could otherwise be avoided. But your prayers will help those who fall victim to evil schemes. Your prayers also bring hope to people who live in places where systems of oppression keep entire classes of people in misery. Every prayer makes a difference. By remembering to take a stand against wrong in your time alone with God, you will make your world a better place.

God, I want to stand against evil. I pray for...

Praying for Unity

Be completely humble and gentle; be patient,
bearing with one another in love. Make every effort
to keep the unity of the Spirit through the bond of peace.
EPHESIANS 4:2–3

What a difference relationships can make! Have you ever been in a group where everyone seems irritable, at each other's throats, insulting one another? Think about how uncomfortable that feels. But being among those who respect, care for, and honor one another creates a much more enjoyable experience. No wonder parents get concerned when siblings squabble.

As you pray, one of the most important things you can seek is unity among those who follow God. The love that we have for one another gives each person a safe place to learn and grow. And as we pray together, our prayers are powerful. But when followers of God are divided, they end up working at cross purposes, and precious energy is wasted on needless quarrels. Jesus considered this so important that it became the main focus of His longest recorded prayer, as found in John chapter 17.

You can touch the heart of God by praying that fellow believers will love one another.

God, I pray for unity in...

Experiencing God

Seek the LORD while he may be found; call on him while he is near.
ISAIAH 55:6

How did you first experience God? What brought you to where you are now? As you think over the story of your life, you may see others around you walking where you once walked. All of us are on a spiritual journey, but not everyone has a relationship with God. Many people are looking for God but haven't come into that settled assurance that you may have that they belong to Him. Others are frantically searching for something but don't comprehend that what they long for is God Himself.

You can make a powerful difference in the lives of others by praying that they will experience God. As you pray that the good news becomes clear for others, God can frame in their minds the steps they need to take to find their way back to Him. Through your prayers, they might find mentors who can help them in their journey.

As you pray and share God's love, you may see many people make that most important discovery—a satisfying relationship with God.

God, I pray for those who haven't discovered You, especially...

Sharing Your Plans

Live out your God-created identity.
MATTHEW 5:48 MSG

God has no desire to squelch you. He enjoys watching you be you. He loves to see you express yourself with choices that follow His pathway of right living and allow you to become the person *you* were created to be.

Just as parents understand that each child is radically different from the next, so God embraces and celebrates your uniqueness. As wise parents allow and encourage each child to develop their own interests and pursue their own dreams, so also God delights in your dreams. In fact, your deepest dreams are planted by Him. They are part of the package that makes you uniquely you. God coaches you and cheers you on.

God's enjoyment of your uniqueness can be celebrated in your prayers, as you take the time to share with Him your dreams, your plans, and your choices and hold them before Him with an open hand. He loves walking with you as you make decisions and choose a path that allows you to be you. Where will you begin to pursue your dreams?

God, the dream I am most excited about is...

God's Healing Perspective

The LORD is close to the brokenhearted and saves those who are crushed in spirit.
PSALM 34:18

Most of us have had the experience of comforting a small child who has experienced physical or emotional pain. A few minutes in the arms of a loving parent or other caring adult is usually enough to soothe a little person's everyday hurts.

In the same way, God longs to comfort us as we experience emotional pain as adults. He invites us to come to Him for reassurance and encouragement as well as healing. But sometimes the pain runs very deep and is held in place by lies that have been believed and closed up inside. In these cases, God wants to replace those painful lies with healing truth during our time of prayer, whether alone with God or with the help of an experienced minister or counselor.

As you pray, don't be afraid to be completely honest with God. He isn't afraid of your strong emotions. As you express to Him what feels true inside, allow Him to enlighten you so that you see things from His healing perspective.

God, some of the lies I want You to replace with Your truth are...

Wisdom and Healing

My whole being, praise the LORD and do not forget all his kindnesses.
He forgives all my sins and heals all my diseases.
PSALM 103:2–3 NCV

What can you do if you or someone you love is sick or in pain? There's much you can do! God is a healing God who designed systems in your body to empower you to recover from illness and heal from injury. In addition, tens of thousands of people all over the world have reported cases of miraculous healing—too many to ignore or discount. Healing comes from God.

How do you pray for healing? The place to start is a prayer for wisdom. God promises to grant wisdom to anyone who sincerely asks for it. As you scour the Bible for insight, you will find many clues that not only may lead to healing, but to a much deeper relationship with God in the process. Armed with that wisdom, you can pray intelligently and effectively. Wisdom will usually shorten the path to healing and recovery. Seek wisdom first and, as a rule, healing will follow.

God, I need wisdom concerning these needs in my life...

....

....

....

....

....

....

....

Beneath the Surface

[Our fathers] disciplined us for a little while as they thought best;
but God disciplines us for our good, in order that we may share in his holiness.
HEBREWS 12:10

When God looks at your life, many things are clearly in focus for Him that may not be on your radar screen at all. Much of life is a process of God bringing those things into focus for you.

When difficulties enter your life, God may use these struggles to bring something to your attention that will greatly help you. Like an Olympic athlete in training, God is training you for the life and the eternity that He has planned for you. While the individual ingredients of your life may not be at all pleasant, the final product will be beautiful. God does not enjoy seeing His children in pain. But He may use that pain to bring something into the light that He wants to discuss with you.

How do you pray through this? Simply ask. Ask God if there's something—anything—that He wants you to see. As you submit yourself to Him, He will show you the way forward.

God, some things I need to bring into focus are...

_____

_____

_____

_____

_____

_____

_____

In the Way

I pray that you may prosper in all things and be in health, just as your soul prospers.
3 JOHN 1:2 NKJV

Are you experiencing the frustration of a chronic disease or other health condition that won't go away? Sometimes these things linger, and prayer and medical treatment seem not to help at all. However, it never hurts to ask God, "Is there anything standing in the way of my healing?" In the Bible, we read of a whole nation that was suffering because they were neglecting justice for the oppressed and kindness to the poor. A prophet assured the people that if these matters were corrected, they would quickly be healed.

As you pray for healing for yourself or others, pause before God and ask Him: "Is there a fault that needs to be corrected? Is there a good deed that needs to be done? Is there a relationship that needs to be mended?"

If God brings something to your attention, you can take action, or, depending on what it is, you can pray more intelligently. Each time you do, you get closer not only to the healing, but to God's perfect plan for your life.

God, the things that might be hindering my prayers are...

Prayer and Community

May the God who gives this patience and encouragement
help you live in complete harmony with each other,
as is fitting for followers of Christ Jesus.
ROMANS 15:5 NLT

As much as God enjoys visiting with you privately, have you considered how important it is to involve others in your life of prayer? Prayer is not only an individual exercise; it is also a matter of community.

One example of this is praying for healing. The Bible instructs followers of God to call for the elders of the church when someone is sick so that they can pray over that person. Why? Involving others is an invitation back into interdependency. As others join with the sick person in prayer, they can help carry the load of intercession.

Even in prayer, you are not an island. Jesus Himself wanted His friends to pray with Him. Sickness, as bad as it is, can be a gateway not only to the healing of the human body but also to the healing of relationships. As you walk together with others in transparency and humility, friendships are restored, marriages are healed, and the community is made whole once again.

God, I would like others in my community to join me in prayer for...

Giving Thanks

Always giving thanks to God the Father for everything,
in the name of our Lord Jesus Christ.
EPHESIANS 5:20

Sometimes doing the right thing can take a great deal of courage. Take giving thanks, for example. It might seem strange to give thanks when you are suffering. The biblical command to offer thanksgiving to God in all circumstances might seem cruel and unfeeling. But the reasons for giving thanks are many.

By focusing on the good, you put your circumstances in their proper perspective. God is love. He will provide healing. You are on the winning team. Thanksgiving is an affirmation that God's presence is sufficient, that you desire God above all other things. As you give thanks, you demonstrate God-honoring faith that encourages others. You gain contentment and patience, making you stronger and more ready for anything life might throw at you. As you persist in giving thanks, the moment may come when your struggle is no longer necessary, and God may remove it.

As you find the courage to thank God despite your feelings, the Bible teaches that you are opening a door for God to act in your behalf.

God, in my current circumstances, I give thanks for...

Affirming God's Goodness

*The righteous keep moving forward, and those
with clean hands become stronger and stronger.*
JOB 17:9 NLT

The Bible devotes forty-two chapters to the story of a man who experienced extraordinary suffering. All his wealth was taken away. He lost his status as a community leader. All ten of his children were suddenly and unexpectedly killed on the same day. While his head was reeling from all of this, he was struck with an ugly and painful skin disease that robbed him of sleep. His friends came to comfort him but ended up telling him over and over again that he must have done something terrible to deserve such a fate. But he hadn't. He had done nothing wrong.

In his prayers, this man argued with God, blamed God, pleaded with God. But finally, in an encounter with God Himself, he came to this settled conclusion: *God is good, even when I can't understand what He's doing.* Prayer is often a journey to that destination. You won't always understand what God is doing in your life. But God is always good.

God, I want to affirm that You are good by...

Best Possible Future

Whoever heeds life-giving correction will be at home among the wise..
PROVERBS 15:31

As you pray for your own needs and those of others, you may be tempted to ask, "Is this circumstance a punishment from God?" The answer is usually no. God is focused on bringing you into the best possible future, not in rubbing your nose in the faults of your past. But God does correct His children. If you are headed in a direction that is not good, God will use whatever means it takes to turn you around. It doesn't hurt to ask God, "Are You correcting me?" And if you are open to His correction, He will usually use a gentle word from someone to put you on the right path.

For example, while some car accidents are unpreventable, others are a consequence of bad choices such as following too closely or ignoring traffic signs. God looks to you to make wise choices in everything you do. But if you're living with consequences of poor decisions, invite God in. Admit your mistakes; enjoy His presence. You never know what He might do.

God, the mistake I need to admit is...

....

....

....

....

....

....

....

Keeping a Balance

Oh, that my steps might be steady, keeping to the course you set.
PSALM 119:5 MSG

If a little bit of prayer is good, more prayer would be better, right? Maybe, but not necessarily. In the Old Testament book of Joshua, we read the story of an army that had suffered defeat. The leader was distraught and fell onto the ground, agonizing in prayer. But God's message came to him: "Get up. What are you doing down on your face? I have a job I want you to do." Even in the story of Adam and Eve, who enjoyed a perfect relationship with God, prayer was not a twenty-four/seven activity. It was part of their daily routine but not the only thing they did.

If you're like most of us, the problem is not too much time spent in prayer. We all need to listen to the Lord and learn from Him how much time to dedicate to prayer. Some people pray an uninterrupted hour or more daily. One famous Christian said, "I never pray more than fifteen minutes, but I never go more than fifteen minutes without praying." God wants your life to be in balance.

God, one structured prayer time I want to honor is...

The Heart of a Leader

*We have different gifts, according to the grace given
to each of us. If your gift is...to lead, do it diligently.*
ROMANS 12:6, 8

Prayer can be a gateway to leadership. When you represent your family, your church, your school, your community, your nation, or some other group of people in your prayers, you are praying as a leader. As you step into God's presence, you cease to advocate for your own interests and instead represent the interests of the entire group.

The Bible contains many examples of leaders praying. In their prayers, they focused on God's promises to their followers, and they thanked God for His history with their people—the work that He had already done. They recognized and confessed the shortcomings of their people (including their own transgressions) and asked for God's cleansing and forgiveness. Then they brought the needs of the people before God.

Praying as a leader takes you to a different level of prayer. As you think like a father or mother, as an advocate, you put the interests of others ahead of your own. This step of maturity prepares you for and flows from a place of leadership.

God, the group of people I care deeply about are...

Seeking Guidance in Prayer

I am continually with You;
You hold me by my right hand.
You will guide me with Your counsel.
PSALM 73:23–24 NKJV

Prayer can be a wonderful way to get God's guidance for your life or for any decision you need to make. When you pray for direction, start with what you already know to be true. Does the Bible provide instruction in the area where you are seeking advice? Have good people spoken words of wisdom into your life?

As you pray, ponder what you've already received. Ask God to give you deeper insight into what you're sure about. Many times the wisdom you need is hidden in plain sight, wrapped up in the truth you already know.

Of course, God only instructs His children as much and as far as they are willing to obey. Getting more guidance from God requires following the instructions already received. If there is reluctance to follow direction you've already received, then the place to start is a conversation with God about that hesitation. As you share your reasons with God, He is able to help you gain His perspective on the best path for you.

God, I need Your guidance concerning...

_____

_____

_____

_____

_____

_____

_____

Not Off Limits

Pray about everything. Tell God what you need, and thank him for all he has done..
PHILIPPIANS 4:6 NLT

No topic is off limits for prayer. When you meet with God in private, any topic you want to explore with Him is open for discussion. The deep reverence you have for God does not exclude certain subjects from your prayer agenda; on the contrary, it invites them.

The safest place to talk about your secret longings, your hidden fears, your dreams of glory, your deepest shame, and all the questions you can't ask anyplace else is in the presence of God. Nothing will shock Him. Nothing will surprise Him. He already loves you with a perfect, boundless love; nothing you say will cause Him to love you any more or any less.

Why talk about these things with God? God wants to relate to the real you, not some religious caricature of yourself. God wants to bring goodness and wholeness to every part of your life. As God's presence fills all the compartments of your life, His strength and peace follows. As your intimacy with God grows, your own sense of well-being will grow with it.

God, what is going on in my head today is...

Gaining God's Approval

*Do not, O Lord, withhold your mercy
from me; let your steadfast love and your
faithfulness keep me safe for ever.*
PSALM 40:11 NRSV

At the time of Jesus, during the height of the Roman Empire, revenue reached the royal coffers through a network of tax collectors. These agents of the state were often little more than thugs and gangsters who made their living by collecting far more than Rome wanted and pocketing the difference.

With this in mind, Jesus defied all the expectations of His culture and used the prayer of a tax collector as a model for those who want to get right with God. The despised revenue man, unable to look heavenward, cried out in anguish, "God be merciful to me, a sinner."

We, too, need to survey the moral distance between ourselves and God, and come face-to-face with reality: We don't measure up. Any merit we hoped to gain from our good deeds looks small and irrelevant when we stand in the presence of a holy God. It is our cry for mercy—our recognition of our own moral bankruptcy—that brings that comforting wave of God's approval—something we cannot gain any other way.

God, be merciful to me concerning...

Aha! Moments

Let the wise also hear and gain in learning, and the discerning acquire skill.
PROVERBS 1:5 NRSV

Sometimes we pray the prayer of experience: "Now I see. Now I get it." This happened to a great pagan king in the biblical narrative. Consumed by his own arrogance, he failed to see how he could use his power to benefit the needy. As a result, God humbled him by causing him to lose his mind for seven years. During that time, he lost his royal position and behaved like a farm animal.

When his sanity was restored and his place of authority returned to him, his first act was to honor God in prayer. He found his place in God's presence, as a servant king, placed on earth to do God's bidding rather than his own.

While the turning points in your life may not be so dramatic, all of us experience *aha!* moments when we see life and our place in it from a new perspective. Prayer is a great opportunity for you to review and anchor yourself to life's lessons. What has God been teaching you? Review it, discuss it, and seal it in prayer.

God, I had an aha! moment when...

Impossible Situations

Rejoice in hope, be patient
in suffering, persevere in prayer.
ROMANS 12:12 NRSV

We all face impossible situations at times. The Bible is full of accounts of real people with needs that they had no way to meet without God's intervention.

One of the more inspiring stories concerns a woman named Hannah, who desperately wanted a son. Nobody understood the depth of her pain. Her husband tried to minimize it. The spiritual leader at the time saw her praying in anguish and mistook her for a drunk. Not knowing what else to do, she turned to God and made a deal with Him. "If You give me a son," she prayed, "I'll give him back to You." God answered her prayer, and she bore a son. Hannah kept her vow to God and gave young Samuel back to God's service. He grew to be a great leader.

Praying about something that seems impossible? Don't give up. Even if no one else understands, God does. Keep on praying. Be creatively persistent. Find another way to pray. Ask for wisdom. Do a spiritual checkup on yourself. But be tenacious. Persevere. The answer you are looking for just might change your world.

God, the thing I need most from You is...

Your Prayer of Triumph

We will shout for joy when you succeed, and we will raise a flag in the name of our God.
PSALM 20:5 NCV

Sooner or later, you win because you are on the winning team—you are a son or daughter of God. Triumph is your destiny. Success is your birthright as a member of God's royal family. That will look a little different for each person, but in the things that really matter, you win.

The great men and women of the Bible remembered that their success came from somewhere outside themselves. In their moment of triumph, they paused to acknowledge God's greatness. When He gives you the victory you desire or grants you the ability you need, remember all of your provision comes from His hand.

If you are in the daily habit of praising God for His goodness in your life, your success will be yet another opportunity to see life from His perspective.

God, because of You, I am triumphant in...

Touchdown

*Whoever heeds discipline shows the way to life,
but whoever ignores correction leads others astray.*
PROVERBS 10:17

When a pilot lands a plane, he lines up his aircraft with the runway miles away from the airport. He calculates the direction, speed, and rate of descent long before he comes in over the runway so the touchdown will be smooth and uneventful. Pilots do this because large course corrections directly over the airport are impossible.

Your life is headed toward a destination. Someday you will stand before God. Like a pilot, you can be prudent and use your prayer time as an opportunity to prepare for that all-important meeting. You can check in with God and ask Him where you stand. This makes perfect sense. In school, you receive report cards. In your place of employment, you receive performance reviews. By regularly asking God where you stand with Him, you have ample opportunity to make any needed course corrections now while you have time to do so.

God wants your "touchdown" with Him to be a time of great joy for you both, made possible because you check in with Him today.

God, where do I stand with You? The area I may need correction in is...

A New Identity

Do not fear, for I have redeemed you;
I have summoned you by name; you are mine.
ISAIAH 43:1

One person in the Bible is known only for his prayer. That person was Jabez. His name meant pain and sorrow. With this identity stamped over his life, he looked heavenward to the only One who could give him a different destiny. Calling out to God, he asked for prosperity and freedom from pain. God granted his request.

What messages have been written over your life? God alone can give you a new name, a new identity, a new future, when you call out to Him.

All of us live with labels. Some of those labels can be extraordinarily negative like "STUPID," "UGLY," "INCOMPETENT," or worse. But God has the power to rip up those labels and make everything new for you. You have a place. You have a role. You have importance.

As you call out to God, He will set you free from the weights that may have held you back all your life. This is the kind of life-transforming God He is.

God, some of the labels I would like to get rid of are...

....

....

....

....

....

....

....

....

It's All in the Struggle

Pursue righteousness, godliness, faith, love, endurance and gentleness. Fight the good fight of the faith.
1 TIMOTHY 6:11–12

In the process of emerging from its cocoon, a butterfly struggles, sometimes for hours, to break free. This struggle forces enzymes from the body into the wing tips, strengthening the muscles and reducing the body weight. As a result, the butterfly can fly. If someone tries to help the butterfly by cutting the cocoon, the insect will emerge but never be able to fly and will quickly die, because the struggle itself opens the door to the freedom of flight.

Sometimes you will travail in prayer, struggling for hours, weeks, or longer, and God won't cut your cocoon for you. You pray, but God seems far away. Your requests seem reasonable, but they go unanswered. You wonder if God has forgotten, or if He's playing some kind of trick on you. Great men and women of God have these kinds of struggles.

When it comes to making you into the person you were designed to be, God doesn't take shortcuts. He values your labor. By persevering in prayer, you will find the freedom you long for.

God, I want to persevere in...

Big God, Small People

*I tell you, whoever believes in me will do...even greater
things than these, because I am going to the Father.*
JOHN 14:12

Have you ever thought that maybe your prayers are too small? A big God inside a small you can still make a huge difference—if you let Him.

Gladys Aylward was a domestic worker in London who dreamed of becoming a missionary to China. Her application was turned down by the mission agency, but that didn't stop her. She booked passage to China anyway and went on to stop a prison riot, start an orphanage and a school, and lead ninety-four orphans to safety during World War II. Books and a Hollywood movie tell the story of her life. What did she have to offer? The willingness to believe that God can use a simple person to accomplish great things.

Don't be afraid to ask God for something great. A big request honors God. Better to be turned down asking for something big than to settle for the scraps of mediocrity. Ask God for what it takes to make your world a better place.

God, my God-sized request is...

Total Dependence

I trust in you, O Lord;
I say, "You are my God."
My times are in your hand.
PSALM 31:14–15 NRSV

God knows the difference between the people who rely on Him and those who merely mouth empty prayers. If you are a parent and your children ask you for food, you provide it if you can. You understand that your children depend on you for sustenance. They trust you to take care of them. You honor their relationship with you and their trust in you by providing for their needs.

Part of the secret of answered prayer is understanding your relationship with God and your dependence on Him. The more you understand that everything comes from God, the easier it will be to totally depend on Him. In the Bible, we see illustrations of how God answers the prayers of those who trust in Him. These people clearly understood that they had nowhere else to turn. This childlike faith and dependence on God is key to answered prayer.

God, I trust You to...

_____

_____

_____

_____

_____

_____

_____

_____

Getting Through

The message of the cross is foolishness to those who are perishing,
but to us who are being saved it is the power of God.
1 CORINTHIANS 1:18

Have you ever felt like you were speaking a foreign language when you tried to talk to one of your friends about God? Sometimes the things that make perfectly good sense to you are pure nonsense to others. You search for words to make yourself clear but find none.

In your times of prayer, ask God to open both your eyes and the eyes of your friends to the truth about Him. Ask Him to allow you to share with them what you have already learned. This will always be a struggle because the enemy of faith in God is always working to nullify your faith and make you look foolish so you will not continue to learn and grow.

Ask God to solidify in your heart those things you have come to believe are true about God. Then ask Him to help you find a way to share those things with others. He will help you in any way He can.

God, when it comes to what I have learned about You, I want to share...

Claiming God's Promises

All of God's promises have been fulfilled
in Christ with a resounding "Yes!" And through Christ,
our "Amen" (which means "Yes") ascends to God for his glory.
2 CORINTHIANS 1:20 NLT

How do you pray for great things? Claim God's great promises. The Bible is filled with promises that God makes to His people.

The popular Twenty-Third Psalm is a good place to start. God is your shepherd. He watches over you. He will take care of your needs. He restores your inner self. He will guide you in ways that are right. Even when you are surrounded by enemies, He will confidently spread a picnic blanket before you, filled with good things. Nothing can keep His love away from you. You will always belong to His family.

One way to claim God's promises is to line up His promises against your feelings of doubt and discouragement. For example, "I feel like I will always be all alone. But Your word says that You set the lonely in families. So I choose to believe that the right relationship is out there, waiting for me."

Claiming God's promises allows you to fight back against faith-quenching doubt and to gain the confidence you need to move forward.

God, the promise I need most right now is...

Being Specific

If you remain in me and my words remain in you,
ask whatever you wish, and it will be done for you.

JOHN 15:7

If you were to send someone to the grocery store to pick up a few items for you, would you say, "Please buy me some groceries"? Or would you say, "I need a gallon of 2 percent milk, a dozen large eggs, and a loaf of whole wheat bread"? Almost certainly, you would be specific about what you wanted because you have meal plans that correspond to your individual needs.

In the same way, when you pray, practice being specific when you are asking for things. A man in Asia desperately needed a bicycle to start a business to support his family, but no matter how hard he prayed he received no bicycle. So he asked God why He wouldn't give him a bike. The answer he felt he got back was this: "You haven't told Me what kind of bicycle you want." So the man got specific with his prayer request. The next day, he had his bicycle.

God delights in fulfilling your exact needs, and satisfying your specific desires with good things.

God, here's exactly what I need...

What You Really Need

*Whoever gathers money
little by little makes it grow.*
PROVERBS 13:11

There are times when what you need from God is simple—money. But is it right to ask Him for it? Absolutely.

God is your provider. He knows that you need money to pay your bills. In your prayers, identify what you need, when you need it, and why you need it. Then look expectantly to Him for an answer. But understand that God might provide those funds in many different ways. Sometimes God provides money in miraculous ways, like cash showing up in your mailbox. But most often God supplies money by giving you a job, a business, or an investment opportunity. And He expects you to use what He gives you prudently.

In whatever way God chooses to provide, you have the privilege of honoring Him with your wealth by remembering others in need and sharing with those who make serving God their full-time profession.

As you see God supply, a deep well of gratitude springs up inside. Even if you don't have the latest and greatest, God grants contentment that no amount of money can buy.

God, my financial needs are...

Under Our Management

The Lord answered, "Who then is the faithful and wise manager,
whom the master puts in charge of his servants to give
them their food allowance at the proper time? It will be good
for that servant whom the master finds doing so when he returns."

LUKE 12:42–43

Technically, none of us owns anything. God owns everything. We simply manage a portion of God's wealth. No prayer for finances would be complete without acknowledging that everything we ask for belongs to God before and after we receive it. Since the money is His, He has the right to tell us how it should be used.

This gives us an enormous amount of freedom. We don't have to own anything. We just take care of God's things for Him. The possessions He has put into our hands become His investments, under our management, to advance His purposes here on earth. That can look very different from moment to moment. It might mean buying an ice cream cone for a child, paying your phone bill, or sending five hundred dollars to a missionary.

If you ask, God will give you the wisdom to manage His possessions well.

God, when it comes to managing Your things, I need help with...

Priorities in Prayer

Set your mind on things above, not on things on the earth.
COLOSSIANS 3:2 NKJV

It's a sign of maturity when we realize that we must set priorities on what we ask of God.

The first priority, of course, is God Himself. By valuing God over His gifts, you keep in mind that the real treasure of eternal life is knowing Him. All of our needs, wants, and desires are ultimately satisfied in Him.

The second priority is people. The eternal well-being of others matters more than projects or ideas or provision or knowledge. We can never go wrong by putting God first and people second. If this is what we're seeking in prayer, we are honoring Him.

The third priority is wisdom. The Bible tells us that wisdom is more precious than wealth. It will keep us on the path God has for us, protecting us and helping us make right decisions. Understanding will guide us into the solution to every problem.

Seek wisdom; make it a lifelong pursuit in your prayers. Your fourth priority will be everything else. God loves answering the prayers of the person who keeps His priorities straight.

God, my priorities in order are...

Giving Back

I will sacrifice a freewill offering to you;
I will praise your name, LORD, for it is good.

PSALM 54:6

Sometimes the best thing you can do with an answer to prayer is to give it back to God.

In the Bible, King David did this when he was in a battle. David longed for water from a well that was behind enemy lines. A couple of his soldiers overheard his request. They personally fought their way to the well, drew out the water, and fought their way back to the King. David was so overwhelmed by this gift that he couldn't bring himself to drink the water. "This is the blood of these men who went at the risk of their lives to bring this gift to me," he said. Instead, he poured the water out as an offering to God.

Even children who have prayed for a toy or a game will sometimes be deeply moved by another child in need and spontaneously give their gift away. This isn't a rule to be followed, but rather a moment of worship. Our answer to prayer can serve a higher purpose than we ever imagined.

God, I want to give these things back to You...

A Firm Foundation

The word of the LORD is right, and all His work is done in truth.
PSALM 33:4 NKJV

God Himself is truth. He isn't *a* truth. He isn't true for some people and not for others. He *is* truth. We know this and can be certain about it because He Himself spoke it. If this statement that He made about Himself is not true, then nothing about Him can be trusted, because humanity would have no way of verifying which of His statements were accurate, which were mistakes, and which were out-and-out fabrications.

That God is true is the reassuring foundation upon which all of our prayers rest. We are praying to the God who is really there. What He promises He will do. He can be trusted with our prayers, our longings, our secrets, our fragile and vulnerable feelings, and even our lives.

When you bow in prayer before God, you aren't merely pointing your thoughts and energies in a positive direction. You are communicating with the God of the universe. As you open the door of your life to God, you are resting on the bedrock of truth.

God, I am trusting You with...

_____

_____

_____

_____

_____

_____

_____

All-Night Prayer

I bless the Lord who gives me counsel; in the night also my heart instructs me.
PSALM 16:7 NRSV

Have you ever pulled an all-nighter? Most of us, at one point or another, have stayed up all night with a sick child or to finish a term paper or work on some project. The Bible records an all-nighter that Jesus pulled. Just prior to choosing the twelve men who became His apostles, Jesus went up into a mountainside and prayed throughout the night.

When you need to make a decision that has far-reaching consequences, you will want to invest extra time in the presence of God. On the very most important choices you make in life, you may even find yourself pulling an all-nighter.

As a rule, the extra time you devote to prayer and pondering God's Word will bring clarity. The correct choice will make itself known. But even if it doesn't, your investment shows your determination to know and follow God's will. Rest assured, He will find a way to protect you in your decision-making process if you remain open to Him.

God, the most important decision I need to make is...

....

....

....

....

....

....

....

....

APRIL 25

Going on the Offensive

Don't retaliate with insults when people insult you.
Instead, pay them back with a blessing.
1 PETER 3:9 NLT

Being mistreated is a painful experience. Whether it's the estrangement of friends due to the actions of a gossip, the feelings of embarrassment or betrayal when someone breaks a confidence, or even physical pain as a result of an assault, pain is not fun. It's often not easy to get over, either. Unfortunately, after our initial reaction subsides, a more permanent pain can set in. We might begin to believe the hurtful lies about ourselves, or allow resentment to smolder within, or nurture an increasingly deep-seated bitterness.

The Bible instructs us to pray when we are mistreated by someone. This may seem like a strange approach, but it is wise. Praying for the person who has mistreated you forces you to tackle the pain head-on. It gives you an opportunity to turn an action meant for evil into something God can use for good.

When you are mistreated, remember this simple and wise strategy. Go to God in prayer. Ask Him to bless the person who has harmed you. As soon as you do, healing begins.

God, my prayer for the person who has mistreated me begins...

God's Love Language

Faith is the substance of things hoped for, the evidence of things not seen.
HEBREWS 11:1 KJV

Prayer is an act of faith. We can't see the God we pray to. Few hear His audible voice. We don't sit down with God the same way we might sit down with a friend and enjoy a cup of coffee. While faith is not at all unreasonable, nor is it inconsistent with an intelligent examination of the facts, it is, nevertheless, faith.

Why is faith essential to prayer? Faith honors God for what He is: wise, loving, reliable, just, and powerful, even when our circumstances seem to contradict those truths. Faith is the bridge that takes us back to God. It is that assurance within that while our five senses are incomplete, an invisible God is indeed present. It is an inner affirmation that declares that God is good even when circumstances are not.

We are encouraged by those who believe in us. Likewise, God is impressed and touched when we trust in Him. Faith is God's love language. And prayer pulls us back into that bridge of faith.

God, build my faith in the area of...

In Line

*I will meditate on your majestic, glorious
splendor and your wonderful miracles.
Your awe-inspiring deeds will be on every tongue.*
PSALM 145:5–6 NLT

Prayer puts you in the path of the supernatural. Many, if not all, of the amazing things that happened in the Bible happened during or as a result of prayer. People were healed. The ocean was parted. The sun stood still. Multitudes were fed. God intervenes when humans intercede.

This doesn't mean that you will always experience something spectacular when you pray. Most of the time you won't. Depending on where you live, most of the time you won't see a fox or a coyote when you take a walk in a nature preserve.

On the other hand, if you don't take the walk, you never will.

Likewise, prayer is usually not spectacular. We're often unaware of what is happening in the spiritual realm.

But if you don't invest in prayer, you won't be there to experience the wonder and the beauty of God doing something out of the ordinary. Your best chance of receiving from God happens if—and only if—you're standing in line waiting on Him.

God, I want to be in line for You. Help me to...

Bigger Than Life

Imitate those who through faith and patience inherit what has been promised.
HEBREWS 6:12

Some prayers will not be answered in your lifetime—and for good reason. The best God has for you cannot fit in a span of seventy or eighty years. It's too big, too good, too wonderful to be realized here in a fallen world.

In the Bible, the great father of faith Abraham died before the great promises of God were realized in his life. His descendants were hardly numberless as God had promised. Instead, they could easily be gathered into a small living room. His family still lived as squatters in the land God promised they would possess. But Abraham never stopped believing, and after his death, all of God's promises came true.

You may be praying for something great, something you feel God has promised. Persevere in your faith. Remember, God is not limited in what He can do. Allow Him room to answer you on a grand scale. God is weaving together human history and eternal life; your prayers are part of the mix, and they will influence the outcome.

God, my bigger-than-life request is...

God's Name

Every word of God is pure: he is a shield unto them that put their trust in him.
PROVERBS 30:5 KJV

Imagine that two people are much in love, but a jealous acquaintance wants to sabotage the relationship. How could she do it? Here's one way: She could spread doubts and rumors. She could convince the woman that the man is a cheat and a liar, that his affections are not really devoted to her. If the woman believes these lies instead of trusting the man's character and affirmations of love, the relationship will suffer.

This is why Jesus instructed His disciples to begin their prayers with "Hallowed be Thy name." Jesus was seeking to protect our relationship with God, by keeping us anchored to the truth. God wants you to know the truth about who He really is and how much He cares about you. His name is His character, His reputation in your heart and on this earth. The name of God must be untarnished, free from lies, and kept sacred.

As you pray, focus on protecting and honoring who God is. Doing this will bring everything—in prayer and in life—into sharper focus.

God, when I think about Your name, my first thought is...

He Cares

Cast your cares on the Lord and he will sustain you; he will never let the righteous be shaken.
PSALM 55:22

One of the best ways to maintain a trusting relationship with God is to remember that He cares. No one hurts without God also hurting. He is thrilled with your success; He weeps when you weep. This is a starting place for understanding and appreciating God.

In your life of prayer, you will intercede for many people who have experienced horrible tragedy. Some people, having traveled to areas of the world where poverty and oppression are severe, have nearly lost their faith, but the truth is that the only thing bigger than human need is the heart of God.

God can and does carry the hurts you cannot carry yourself. He will allow you to make a difference with your prayers, your gifts, and your service. But He won't overwhelm you with pain that you are not able to handle. The world is messed up, but God is not. He responds appropriately to every human hurt while remaining strong, loving, and ready to help.

God, the hurts I want to give to You are...

Having Fun

Surely you have granted him unending blessings and made him glad with the joy of your presence.
PSALM 21:6

Sometimes God is portrayed as a killjoy. But nothing could be further from the truth. Having fun is one of God's specialties.

Jesus spent a good part of His time going to parties, relaxing, and enjoying life. He knew how to joke around. God rejoices over His children with singing. While God is at home with sorrow and pain, He doesn't camp there. He is, deep inside, happy. He measured everything at the beginning and decided it was worth it all. Heaven is heaven for God as well as man. God deeply enjoys His children, His creation, His own eternal life.

When you pray, you are praying to a God who is happy. He is filled with joy. And He is capable of enjoying life with you. He likes hanging out with you. He's not uptight. He's not hyper spiritual all the time. He knows when to get serious, and He knows when to relax and have fun. If you could see His face right now, more likely than not, He would be smiling.

God, thinking of having fun with You makes me feel...

....

....

....

....

....

....

....

God Rules Over All

The LORD has established his throne in heaven, and his kingdom rules over all.
PSALM 103:19

Nothing takes God by surprise. While He allows free choice, nothing ever happens that He can't handle. The Bible says that God has prepared His throne in heaven and His kingdom rules over all. While rebellion occurs, there are no uprisings that He cannot and will not put down. There's a theological term for this: God is sovereign. He works out everything for His purposes—even the evil choices of evil men.

This means that there is no situation that you can present to God in prayer that He cannot do something about. He can always come up with some kind of creative alternative that will bring good out of bad. God rules. Everyone answers to Him. His power is unlimited. He never runs out of solutions. He knows what to do. No problem is too big for God.

You can bring entire nations before Him in prayer, and He can do something that will make a difference. As you pray, pray with the assurance that God will triumph in the end.

God, Your sovereignty assures me that...

Bridging the Gap

Christ Jesus died for us and was raised to life for us, and he is sitting
in the place of honor at God's right hand, pleading for us.
ROMANS 8:34 NLT

Did you know that while you are praying to God, Jesus is praying for you? Your peace with God and your position in heaven are constantly being challenged by the forces of evil. But Jesus intercedes for you.

If you've ever felt unworthy, Jesus is there, reminding God that He is worthy on your behalf. If you've ever felt like you haven't done enough, Jesus is there assuring God that He did enough, He paid the price for you. In His prayers, Jesus is like a defense attorney representing His client before heaven's highest court. Because He stands there defending you, He makes it possible for you to freely walk into God's presence as His much-loved child.

Without someone bridging the gap, there would be a great distance between us and God. God is holy; we are not. But Jesus speaks to God on our behalf, making the easy conversation of prayer an everyday reality.

Jesus, pray for me concerning...

_____

_____

_____

_____

_____

_____

_____

Haughty Eyes

*You save the humble, but your eyes are
on the haughty to bring them low.*

2 SAMUEL 22:28

Did you know that God laughs out loud at certain human beings? While God would never laugh at His own precious children, He does mock the haughty, especially those who think they can use their great earthly power to overthrow God's reign over them.

In your prayers, you will sooner or later come face-to-face with people of power who oppress God. These are oppressors who left on an ego trip and never came back—the Hitlers and Stalins of history who seem to reappear in every generation. It can be very disheartening to intercede for those caught in their grip until you remember that God is not cornered by despots. Their arrogance doesn't faze your God. He is supremely confident in His own certain victory.

As you pray, let your faith rise as you remember that the humble will be exalted, and the proud and evil will not be allowed to prevail.

God, I want to see the world's oppressors through Your eyes so I can...

MAY 5

Coming Home

The Lord is far from the wicked,
but he hears the prayer of the righteous.
PROVERBS 15:29 NRSV

God has the power to—at any moment—say, "Enough!" With a single word, He can bring oppression to an end. He can send the wicked away and rescue those who trust in Him.

But He pauses, eagerly waiting for those who have strayed to find their way back to Him. That is His desire. Every moment He seeks those who have lost their way. Every day He extends another opportunity to let go of rebellion and embrace His leading, His presence, His redemption.

This is where your prayers partner with what God is doing on this earth. As you pray for those who are far from Him, you are becoming part of the solution against evil. In the story of the prodigal son, the young man who squandered his inheritance and ended up in the gutter came to his senses. You can pray that those who are far from God will come to their senses. Only heaven will measure the results of your prayers.

God, when I think about those who are far from You, I pray...

You Might Be the Answer

The one who plants and the one who waters
have a common purpose, and each will
receive wages according to the labor of each.
1 CORINTHIANS 3:8 NRSV

Did you know that you might be the answer to your own prayer?

Bob Pearce, the founder of World Vision, was overwhelmed by the suffering of children in Asia. Challenged to take care of one needy child, he started a ministry that has helped millions. In the same way, you might be the answer to the cry of your heart on behalf of someone else. It might be your dollars, your act of courage, your deed of compassion, your service, or your sacrifice that will bring the answer that you seek.

Never underestimate the power of God to work through you. As a general rule, God answers prayer though human beings—not superstars, but normal people just like you. As you pray, be sensitive to the voice of God's Spirit in your heart. He may be offering you a direct role in meeting that need you care so much about. You may be the one who carries God's presence into a place of desperate need.

God, one need I care passionately about is...

MAY 7

Remembering

I will consider all your works and
meditate on all your mighty deeds.
PSALM 77:12

Each of us has a history with God. He may have brought healing—physical or emotional—into your life. He may have brought you out of a financial scrape. He may have given you courage when you were afraid. He may have spoken words of wisdom into your life when you weren't sure which way to turn. Or He may have helped a friend of a loved one who was in trouble.

In your prayers, you can build on that history. In the Bible, David often made reference to his own history with God when he was praying. Doing so helped him trust in God for the next step in his journey.

We all need reminders. As you pause to remember what God has done for you, your faith grows and becomes ready for the next challenge. Your story will help you when you pray and it will also encourage others who are trying to find their own way forward with God. Each chapter in your life with God opens the door to the next.

God, a few of the things You have done for me are...

....

....

....

....

....

....

....

....

MAY 8

Prayer at Bedtime

May these words of mine,
which I have prayed before the Lord,
be near to the Lord our God day and night.
1 Kings 8:59

You probably have some kind of bedtime routine that might include brushing your teeth, putting on pajamas, reading a book, for example. All of this is a great way to prepare your mind and body for sleep. How about adding prayer to your bedtime routine?

As you pray at night, you hand God all the loose ends of your day. Unresolved problems and questions can be left in His hands. Sometimes you might even awaken with the solution. God often speaks to us in our sleep. God may instruct you to do something before you go to sleep—deliver an apology or carry out some other task. Always obey. Our loving heavenly Father does this so that your sleep will be peaceful.

Prayer at bedtime is a powerful practice. It resets your life, puts your mind at rest, and prepares you for a better tomorrow.

God, the pieces of my life that I want to hand You tonight are...

....

....

....

....

....

....

....

Boundless Love

Come now, let us argue it out, says the LORD: though your sins are like scarlet,
they shall be like snow; though they are red like crimson, they shall become like wool.
ISAIAH 1:18 NRSV

If you feel like you've been mistreated by God, you are not alone. Many of the great men and women of God in the Bible and throughout the ages were bewildered at times by their Creator and His treatment of them. The great prophet Jeremiah said to God, "You tricked me!" Other biblical greats complained that God wouldn't listen to them or that He was sending them trouble for no reason.

What all of these superstars had in common was this: They took their complaint to God Himself in prayer. "I don't understand You," they said. Feeling confused or even hurt by God is part of the human experience.

The best way to resolve that inner turmoil is to lay it out on the table and allow God to respond. He will show you what you need to know. Everything that is now dark will be brought into the light. In the end, you will see that God's love for you knows no bounds.

God, the way I feel about You is...

....

....

....

....

....

....

....

....

MAY 10

Scattered Thoughts

Jesus said, "The mouth speaks what the heart is full of.
A good man brings good things out of the good stored up in him."
MATTHEW 12:34–35

Many people think of prayer as some kind of polished prose, an eloquent speech made in the presence of Almighty God. For the most part, it's anything but that. Prayer is the honest utterance of the human soul. It's the rambling that comes from deep within. It's bunny trails and half sentences, scattered thoughts and long bouts of silence. It resists formula. It's as unique and individual as a fingerprint.

While God deserves your respect, He isn't asking for an essay when you pray. If you get tongue-tied or can't quite figure out how to say what's in your heart, you don't lose any prayer points with God. In fact, the best prayers may not have any words at all, just tears or laughter, a nod, a smile.

Getting real with God is the thing that matters most when you pray. The words you choose to get there are much less important. God cares about you. He wants you as you really are, scattered thoughts and all.

God, some of my scattered thoughts are...

....

....

....

....

....

....

....

Look Heavenward

He counts the number of the stars; He calls them all by name.
PSALM 147:4 NKJV

There's something about looking into the night sky on a clear night that puts things into perspective. To pay a visit to the closest star outside our sun using the fastest speed ever achieved would take nineteen thousand years. But some of the stars we see are a thousand times farther away. It would take nineteen million years to reach them. And then, of course, we're just exploring our corner of our galaxy. There is so much more we simply can't see.

But the galaxies are to God what blocks are to a little child. The God to whom you pray called all of these stars into being. He has a name for each one. We could travel nineteen million years, arrive at our destination, and discover that God is already there. He has been there from the beginning.

When your problems seem way too big and your life feels out of control, look heavenward. Count the stars. Consider the distance. The constellations you see are but a tiny illustration of the unlimited power of your God.

God, when I consider the stars, I am reminded that...

_____

_____

_____

_____

_____

_____

_____

_____

All Around You

Walk out into the fields and look at the wildflowers.
MATTHEW 6:28 MSG

Have you watched hawks soar, riding the thermals in great easy circles in the sky? Have you seen the leaves of the cottonwood tree dance in a summer breeze? There's something about nature that brings the presence of God near. His signature is everywhere—in the moonlight sparkling on the water, in the wildflowers jostling each other in the wind, the trails leading off into the woods. As you walk with God, marveling at His creation all around you, you get a sense of His giddy joy in His work.

It's renewing to drink in the beauty of all living things. This is probably why so many people choose beaches and mountains and parks as vacation destinations.

Give yourself an opportunity to enjoy the outdoors where and when you can. As you do, invite God into the experience. Make it a different kind of prayer—one where requests are not so much on the agenda, but rather quiet enjoyment of each other and of God's artistry. You will walk away enriched and restored.

God, open my eyes to better appreciate...

Elder Perspectives

The quiet words of the wise are more to be heeded than the shouting of a ruler among fools.
ECCLESIASTES 9:17 NRSV

With experience comes a certain perspective. Someone who has walked with God for awhile has had opportunities to see that His ways make sense over the long run.

One productive way to learn more about prayer is to spend time praying with someone who has more life experience than you do. As you pray, listen carefully to the perspectives that person brings to the table. If you have a mentor, even better; you can discuss those prayers and glean valuable insights from them.

Having a more experienced friend pray with you can sometimes bring a sense of stability to a tumultuous moment in your life. You may find that someone more experienced has already weathered the storm you are facing and can see through to the other side.

There is no substitute for the wisdom that comes with age and experience. It can't be bought at any price. When you have added that element, you have truly increased the power and productivity of your prayers.

God, I'm grateful for the people You've put in my life, like...

When Others Triumph

Rejoice with those who rejoice.
ROMANS 12:15

The more you can rejoice in someone else's triumph, the easier it will be for you to intercede for others. There will be times when you are in financial need and God answers your prayers for someone else's material success while you remain in a financial crisis. There will be times when someone else is healed in response to your prayers while you remain sick.

Part of the secret of rejoicing when others rejoice is to let yourself be loved by God. If His answers for others cause you to feel resentment, bring your hurts to Him. Let Him soothe and comfort you. With your own tank full of His love, it's much easier to look around at the needs of others and want good to flow into their lives, while being patient with the burden that you, for the time being, carry.

As you pray for others, imagine their prosperity. Visualize their victory. Feel the happiness they will feel as they experience the full measure of the love of God in their lives. Let yourself go on their behalf, hoping and longing for every good thing for them.

God, I want to rejoice when others win because…

Giving God Room

It is God who is at work in you,
enabling you both to will and to work for his good pleasure.
PHILIPPIANS 2:13 NRSV

Sometimes we don't know what is best for another person. But God does. In your prayers, you can honor God and others by leaving the door open for God to act as He wishes. For example, rather than praying that your son will go out for football, pray that he will discover his God-given strengths and desires and have opportunity to cultivate them.

Each person's spiritual journey is unique. The things that helped you most in your walk with God might not necessarily help the next person. God deals with each person individually.

As you pray for others, you may think they need a certain experience or a particular teaching—and they may—but by giving God room to work with them in His own way, you acknowledge that your experience isn't the template for everyone. With this in mind, you will see faster and more lasting results with your prayers.

God, help me leave the door open for You when I pray for...

MAY 16

Open Eyes

My eyes are fixed on you, Sovereign LORD;
in you I take refuge.
PSALM 141:8

In the Bible we read the account of a prophet who was surrounded by an enemy army. The prophet had a servant who was understandably terrified to be in that situation. So the prophet prayed a simple prayer: "Lord, open his eyes." The servant's eyes were opened to see what he couldn't see before: a great army of angelic beings surrounding the enemy army.

Many times, the goal of your prayers is that your own eyes or someone else's would be opened. As limited human beings, we cannot see life and circumstances from God's perspective unless we see through His eyes. When we see the way God sees, fears dissolve into peace, confidence rises, and direction becomes clear.

If you're praying for healing or a financial breakthrough or any of a thousand other requests, seeing the situation with eyes that are opened by God allows you to pray confidently, intelligently, and patiently.

God, please open my eyes to see as You see concerning...

....

....

....

....

....

....

....

Spiritual Check-Up

You have searched me, LORD, and you know me.
You know when I sit and when I rise; you perceive my thoughts from afar.
PSALM 139:1–2

Many people go to the doctor's office every year for a physical check-up. But it's hard to say how many go for a spiritual check-up. King David did. "Search me," he prayed, "examine me. See what's inside me." By inviting God to give him an honest assessment, David put himself in a much stronger position than he otherwise would have been.

The nice thing about being examined by God is that He doesn't overwhelm you. Even if you were failing, He would zero in on the one thing that you could do to find your way to a better place. God understands that the process of change takes time. He frames one or two choices for you, not a hundred. His motive is love; His method is encouragement. Even in correction, He is kind.

Ask God in prayer to examine you, to run you through His battery of tests. When it's over, you will be in a stronger place.

God, when I think about You examining me, I feel...

One Thing

One thing I asked of the LORD, that will I seek after; to live in the house of the LORD
all the days of my life, to behold the beauty of the LORD, and to inquire in his temple.
PSALM 27:4 NRSV

In the Bible, King David expressed his greatest desire this way: "I want to live in God's house. I want to be near Him. I want to stand there, lost in His beauty." In so doing, he was reflecting the heart cry of men and women of God throughout the ages.

What is the one thing that matters most? Putting God first! Let this one thing occupy your thoughts and your prayers. This is worthy of your devotion, your attention, and your investment. When the famous evangelist D. L. Moody heard these words: "The world has yet to see what God will do with and for and through and in and by the man who is fully consecrated to Him," he determined, "By the grace of God, I will be that man."

If you're focused on a single purpose, you will go far. Seek God first, and everything else you desire will fall into place. Focus on God, and watch everything in your life be transformed.

God, my one desire is...

Sing a New Song

He put a new song in my mouth,
a song of praise to our God. Many people will see
this and worship him. Then they will trust the LORD.
PSALM 40:3 NCV

Have you ever made up a song to God? One of the invitations the Bible extends is this: Sing to the Lord a new song. Parents understand what a treasure this can be. A happy and contented child will sometimes break into song—a new song, spontaneous, from the heart.

Even if you have no musical talent, you can still sing to God when you're alone with Him. Song captures human emotion and experience in a way that words alone cannot. Your song could express whatever is going on inside you—quiet contentment, a deep longing, righteous indignation, or joyful celebration. No one will judge your vocal performance, so you can be free to unselfconsciously sing out whatever is deep inside.

Your song might be the gateway to a whole new dimension of experiencing God. Go ahead! Let the lyrics come and offer them up to God.

God, when I think about singing to You, the words I want to sing are...

A Place to Call Home

Though my father and mother forsake me,
the LORD will receive me.
PSALM 27:10

The struggle with abandonment and isolation is everywhere in our culture today. One little girl wrote about her parents' impending divorce, "I don't know where I will live, but I hope I will be able to see both of them." Cast adrift on a sea of broken relationships, many people are searching for home, for family, for a sense of belonging. These primal needs go unsatisfied until we forge a relationship deep enough to wash away the hurts of the past and usher in the contentment and completion that come from belonging.

When you invite God to be the leader of your life, you gain far more than a new set of priorities. You find your way home. Prayer is a celebration of your position as a child of God. One biblical writer said that, although his father and mother had forsaken him, God had taken him in. God welcomes you with open arms and gives you a place, your own place, in the family of God. No one can take that away.

God, to me being Your child means...

God's Goodness

The LORD is good, a refuge in times of trouble.
He cares for those who trust in him.
NAHUM 1:7

The answer you've been seeking in prayer might not appear right away, but of this you can be sure: You will see God's goodness in the end.

God is good. The world is filled with problems, but God will outlast them all. Just as a matter of statistical probability, the longer you spend time with God, the more likely it is that you will experience the goodness that may be missing from your life.

If your life is totally messed up, how long will it take before you experience the goodness of God? Will you find what you're looking for in an hour? Maybe not. In a day? Possibly. In a year? Probably. In a lifetime? Almost certainly. But God doesn't stop with a lifetime. He offers the gift of eternal life, because the goodness He has for you can't fit in a smaller package.

Keep on praying! Don't give up. You will experience God's goodness if you just give it time.

God, grant me the power to persevere in Your goodness concerning...

What You've Already Won

*How abundant are the good things that you
have stored up for those who fear you, that you bestow
in the sight of all, on those who take refuge in you.*

PSALM 31:19

Imagine winning a million dollars. Even if you were having a terrible day, the news would brighten your spirits. You might not be able to stop jumping up and down. But would all your problems be solved?

Winning a million dollars could be an awesome experience. But something even better is available to you every day: a visit from God. When God shows up, everything changes. The darkest depression disappears in the brightness of His presence. Tears of mourning give way to song and dance. Anxiety turns to peace; anger to laughter; fear to courage. In an instant, everything changes.

Prayer is your invitation for God to invade your world. You can ask for a visit from Him any time. No matter what problem you face, His presence is the answer. As you pray, take God to the deepest, darkest place you can find. Look heavenward. Expect the unexpected. Get ready for everything to change.

God, when You arrive, everything changes. I invite You in to...

God Unshackled

I came to give life—life in all its fullness.
JOHN 10:10 NCV

Religion is way too small to contain our God. It may surprise you to discover that God Himself is not at all churchy. He's real. He hangs out where people are. While He can sometimes be found in church buildings, He can also be found in restaurants, on construction sites, in schools, and in your own living room. God wants to be at the center of everything. He wants to be where you are.

This doesn't mean that God wants to turn all of life into a church service. On the contrary, He rejoices in a great game of football, a quiet chat over coffee with a friend, an honest and energetic sales campaign, a good legal argument, or in whatever makes up the stuff of your life.

Prayer is the transportation system that gets God out of church and into life. By committing every part of your life to Him, by welcoming Him into everything through your prayers, you bring God back to where He belongs, as God and leader of all.

God, my life as I really live it looks like...

MAY 24

Seeking Vindication

A good name is more desirable than great riches;
to be esteemed is better than silver or gold.

PROVERBS 22:1

Building a good reputation can take half a lifetime. Destroying it can take an afternoon. We rightfully value our standing in the community, but we cannot completely control it. Even good people can get a bad name through no fault of their own. When victimized by gossips, unscrupulous journalists, or others who poison your reputation for pleasure or profit, how do you fight back? What do you do?

God is intimately interested in vindicating you. He understands what it means for a good name to be dragged through the mud—it happens to Him every day. Here God invites you to engage Him in prayer, to hand the torn shreds of your reputation over to Him. He offers comfort. He provides wise counsel. And He alone has the power to cause the world to know the truth.

This is not an easy lesson in prayer. It requires patience, prudence, and an understanding that smear campaigns are regularly carried out against good people. But, in the end, God will see that they do not prevail.

God, when I put my reputation in Your hands, I...

MAY 25

Second Chances

*All have sinned and fall short of the glory of God,
and are justified freely by his grace through the redemption that came by Christ Jesus.*
ROMANS 3:23–24

All of us blow it from time to time. We all mess up. We all fail. We do stupid things and wish we could press the DELETE button, but we can't.

Fortunately, God believes in second chances. No matter how badly you may have fallen, God has a perfect plan for the rest of your life. It's a new day. God has a fresh start for you. God doesn't expect you to be perfect—He knows you aren't. He bases His plan on His own perfection. He knows

that it is His presence, not your performance, that transforms an ugly past into a beautiful future. We all need to go to God and admit our mistakes. But God is quick to forgive, and He will always show us a way out.

The path to a new beginning is only a prayer away. This isn't the time to hide. Come out into the open before God. Frankly confess your error. God will show you the way into a better tomorrow.

God, when I blow it, help me...

Celebrate God

Let all who take refuge in you be glad; let them ever sing for joy.
Spread your protection over them, that those who love your name may rejoice in you.
PSALM 5:11

What do you celebrate? Birthdays, anniversaries, Super Bowl victories, promotions? Any of a thousand milestones in life—large and small—can be celebrated as special occasions.

Celebration and holidays go hand in hand. In fact, the word "holiday" comes from the phrase "holy day." Days were holy because they were set apart for God. Traditional holy days such as the Jewish holiday of Passover and the Christian holiday of Christmas commemorate the history of God's involvement in the world of men.

But you don't need a special day to celebrate God. You can throw Him a party in your heart any time you want. Sometimes that's as simple as looking up and smiling. Sometimes you might want to get together with a group of friends, share a meal, sing some songs, and pray together. In your prayers, make room to ponder all that He means to you and let yourself enjoy the presence of God.

God, the thing I celebrate about You is...

MAY 27

Getting Clarity

I am the LORD your God, who teaches you what is best for you,
who directs you in the way you should go.
ISAIAH 48:17

Life can be confusing, to say the least. In the course of any given day, you will have countless choices and literally hundreds of decisions to make. That's why it's so important to be a person of prayer.

God promises to give us guidance whenever we ask for it. That usually doesn't mean an audible voice, but it does mean God is willing and able to place good people in our lives—people who have wisdom to share. He has also given us the Bible and urges us to grow familiar with its principles, for they consistently lead to good. God has also given us His Holy Spirit, whose job it is to give us discernment and to light the path before us.

Yes, life is confusing. But God has broken through the confusion and provided many avenues to gain clarity. Go to Him when you are feeling uncertain. Ask for His help, and He will see that you receive what you need.

God, please help me make decisions about...

....

....

....

....

....

....

....

Easy Clay

LORD, you are our Father. We are the clay, you are the potter;
we are all the work of your hand.
ISAIAH 64:8

Part of the path to maturity is figuring out when to bend and when to stand firm. Sometimes you need to hold your course no matter what kind of opposition you face. At other times, you need to recognize when it's time to give in and let someone else have their way.

In God's hands, you want to be pliable, easy clay for Him to work with, so He can fashion your life into a beautiful masterpiece. But when you stand against the forces of evil, you want to be as hard as rock, unbendable, unshakable. In the Bible, God commends those who tremble at His word. This doesn't mean that they are afraid that God will be abusive. Rather, it means that they are eager to drink in and follow God's instructions.

As you pray, ask God to give you the right combination of backbone and flexibility, of standing firm for Him, yet easily submitting to His direction.

I want to be more pliable in Your hands, God. Help me to...

God's Refrigerator

I bow my knees before the Father, from whom every family in heaven and on earth takes its name.
EPHESIANS 3:14–15 NRSV

One of the pleasures of parenting is receiving artwork and other creations from our children. These masterpieces may be gaudy in the eyes of others, but to a loving mom or dad they are treasures. Displayed with pride on refrigerators, they are a daily reminder that our children are growing up. They are also a sign of belonging, that each child's work has a place, an important place in a family.

As a member of God's family, there is a "refrigerator" in God's "kitchen" for the display of your works. Your acts of kindness, your sacrificial investment in others, your devotion to excellence—all of these things have value to God. As you hold these things up to God, handing them over to Him with the abandon of a child, He takes them and treasures them. They are offerings that bring a smile to God.

In your prayers, commit to God what you've done and what you plan. His affirmation and encouragement will be with you.

God, I most want to give You...

Help Me Listen

My dear friends, you should be quick to listen and slow to speak.
JAMES 1:19 CEV

Before you meet or talk with other people, one of the best things you can pray for is a listening ear. Listening to others validates and affirms them. It is the key that unlocks the door to relationship. You might have wonderful advice for someone, but only by listening to them do you pave the way for a teachable moment when you can share what you know. By listening much and talking less, your words skyrocket in value with those around you.

As you pray for the ability to listen, remember to ask God to open your ears to the whisper of His Spirit. While you meet with others or go about your day, God may have words of encouragement or wisdom to share with you, some of which you can share with others. Keep in mind that God often speaks through other people, and His words to you may come from the lips of a friend, coworker, or someone else.

Much can be done without uttering a word once we learn to listen.

God, help me to listen to You. Show me how to...

Fear or Trust?

Those who know the LORD trust him,
because he will not leave those who come to him.
PSALM 9:10 NCV

There are two kinds of relationships: those built on fear and those built on trust. God wants to banish fear from your life and send you on a prayer journey founded on trust.

If you think of God only as the keeper of the rules, your relationship may be one of fear. But if God is your best friend, if you feel safe with Him and He inspires you to aim high and want the best, then your relationship may be grounded in trust. For most people, it's a little of both.

But as you move toward trust, you discover that God is good, and His ways are better than any you could imagine. You find that you belong. Everything you do flows out of the love you've experienced from Him. Then your prayers take on a whole new dimension. God is more than a judge. He is your friend, and you can trust Him to always have your best interests at heart.

God, guide me into a relationship of trust with You through...

Two Rules for Prayer

LORD, who may dwell in your sacred tent?
Who may live on your holy mountain? The one whose walk is blameless,
who does what is righteous, who speaks the truth from their heart.
PSALM 15:1–2

There really are only two rules for prayer: Be real. Be respectful. Respect matters because human arrogance prevents God from showing up. And honesty connects a supernatural God with real life.

People add advice and formulas to what is, at its heart, a very simple process. Go to God with who you really are and what you're really experiencing. Treat Him with respect. That doesn't mean you need to be fake; on the contrary, even the great biblical hero, Moses, told God more than once that he wished he could die. He asked God to leave him alone. But because he was so straight with God, they enjoyed an unprecedented face-to-face relationship.

The many books and teachings on prayer can be helpful. You will learn ways to go deeper with God, to get breakthroughs, and so on. You will be inspired to pray in new and better ways. But, when the smoke clears, things happen when the real you encounters the real God.

God, I want to be real with You about...

Praying Through Grief

My comfort in my suffering is this:
Your promise preserves my life.
PSALM 119:50

Grief and loss enter everyone's life sooner or later. As a person of prayer, you have your relationship with God to fall back on during these difficult times.

God is the God of all comfort, and He understands sorrow. His heart aches when you are hurting. He will be with you when others can't. He alone stands on both sides of life and death. He alone has the power to wipe every tear and offer you hope and a future even in time of loss.

Anger is one of the natural stages of grief. It's very common to be angry with God, and it is okay and even healthy to share that anger with Him. God is not afraid of your anger. He is not put off by it. As you pour out your heart to Him and find the edges of that anger, He can help you find the comforting truth that goes deeper than your loss, and He will ultimately point the way back to joy.

God, when I experience grief, help me...

Starting With a Dream

May [the LORD] give you the desire of your heart and make all your plans succeed.
PSALM 20:4

From the bubbling cauldron of our daydreams come ideas, dreams, vision, goals, steps, action plans, schedules, and achievements. But it all starts with a daydream—a passing fantasy, a "what if" that floats through our minds.

What a strategic moment to connect with God! As the first inkling of a dream comes together in your mind, you can bounce it off the God who thinks and dreams big, and sees the ramifications of every idea that pops into your brain. As you share your dreams with God, He can shape them and show you even more interesting ways to look at the same challenge or possibility. He will give you wisdom about when and how to connect with resources and other people to help move your dream forward. He will help you know which ideas are worth pursuing and which need to be tabled.

God specializes in taking great ideas and making them work. He loves the process of imagining a better future and of making the plans that move that imagination into reality.

God, what if...

Thirst for God

Let them give thanks to the LORD...
for he satisfies the thirsty
and fills the hungry with good things.
PSALM 107:8–9

Do you ever feel restless? Unsatisfied? Unfulfilled longings are a common human experience. But at the heart of every longing is a thirst for God. No matter what you desire, your desires can only be ultimately satisfied in Him. In fact, He promises to satisfy your desires with good things. A life partner, a new car, a different job, a better marriage—all these things can be good, but only God gives the kind of foundational contentment that makes all of life bearable.

The Bible describes followers of God who suffered imprisonment and all sorts of persecution as being filled with an indescribable joy. How is that possible? It isn't, apart from God. When your thirst for God is satisfied, nothing else matters.

Reach out to God in prayer. As He fills up all the empty places in your heart, His love will overflow to others, even to the unlovable; His joy will bubble up, even in the midst of grief; His peace will guard you, even when you are surrounded by turmoil.

God, I thirst for...

A Voyage of Wonder

Present your bodies as a living sacrifice, holy and acceptable to God, which is your spiritual worship.
ROMANS 12:1 NRSV

In a sense, all of life is a prayer, a voyage of discovery, if you allow it to be. If you throw open the doors to let God in, you will find that you want to live every moment, waking or sleeping, as a love offering to Him. This need not be overly mystical. Rather, it's as practical as saying, "Here I am. My life belongs to You. I give this day to you."

The Bible encourages this kind of prayer when it instructs us to present ourselves as a living sacrifice to God. For some people, this is challenging because they focus on what they give up: their right to be the final authority in their lives. But for others, this is pure joy, their life's highest calling: an opportunity to delight the heart of God Himself.

If you have trouble handing God the keys to your life, ask God to reveal who He is to you. With each new glimpse of His beauty, you'll want to give Him more of yourself. And life will become a voyage of wonder and discovery.

God, I believe deep inside that You really are...

Mercy

Be merciful, just as your Father is merciful.
LUKE 6:36

A pastor and radio personality was fond of saying, "My prayer is that I will be a man of mercy." He went on to explain that God promises leniency to those who show compassion to others. "I need mercy," he added.

If you find it difficult to show mercy, prayer can be a way to grow in empathy. As you intercede for others, you begin to see things from their perspective. See if you can identify what motivates the people you are praying for to act the way they do. This will add understanding and appreciation for those in question.

In many respects, people are all alike. Everyone wants to be loved and respected. Nearly everyone wants a measure of security and an opportunity for self-expression. By praying for others, you will find those points you have in common with them and be better able to celebrate differences.

Do you want to win favor with others? Pray for them, and let your life be characterized by compassion.

God, help me to empathize with...

....

....

....

....

....

....

....

The Missing Puzzle Piece

Our struggle is not against flesh and blood, but against the rulers,
against the authorities, against the powers of this dark world
and against the spiritual forces of evil in the heavenly realms.

EPHESIANS 6:12

In the process of trying to make your world a better place, it is natural to run into opposition and a certain amount of discouragement. This is where prayer can make all the difference in the world.

There is a spiritual dimension to life, and often things need to be prepared in that spiritual dimension before significant changes can take place on other levels. For example, if you're praying for a couple in a troubled marriage, your prayers make it possible for certain kinds of spiritual obstacles to be moved out of the way so understanding can come.

Whether you're volunteering at a food pantry or sending a support check to a sponsored child, your prayers give your efforts more weight and more effectiveness. If things aren't coming together, prayer is often the missing puzzle piece. When you meet with God, a catalyst is added to the mix, and amazing things begin to happen.

God, prepare the way for my efforts concerning...

Your Hiding Place

In you my soul takes refuge; in the shadow of your wings I will take refuge,
until the destroying storms pass by.
PSALM 57:1 NRSV

Have you ever wished you could just get away and hide? All of us need that temporary vacation from the stress of life from time to time. We need a place to regroup, to get our bearings, to get refueled and inspired for the next step in our journey.

God can be your hiding place. He wants to be your refuge during the storms of life. As you hand your cares over to Him, He comforts and calms you. But you need to make the choice to go to Him to find the renewal you need.

As life comes crashing in all around you, reach out to God in prayer. Let yourself slow down long enough to take time to give Him your concerns so He can carry them for you. You may spend a lot of time giving to other people; allow God to give to you. Take a mini vacation with God. You will emerge stronger, more focused, and ready to take on the challenges of your life.

God, the storm in my life right now is...

....

....

....

....

....

....

....

....

....

....

....

June 9

See as God Sees

He has put his angels in charge of you to watch over you wherever you go.
PSALM 91:11 NCV

How would you like to peek straight down from above at your home? You can, instantly. There are several Internet sites that allow you to view the latest available satellite camera photos of your city, even your own house. All you have to do is type in your address, and there it is. It's fascinating, and a bit eerie.

But what man can do with technology, God does far better. Right now, the Lord of heaven and earth is looking down, keeping watch over you! Can you picture it? He's not an indifferent spectator. God cares about and literally gazes upon those who serve Him. His all-seeing, all-knowledgeable character is always awake, ever at work in the lives of the men, women, and children He created. It's simply amazing!

Today, you have a great opportunity. Choose two people to pray for—people you know need God's watchful care. Pray that these people would see Him and discover the destiny He has just for them.

God, two people I feel need Your watchful care are...

JUNE 10

Recovering from Failure

My grace is sufficient for you, for My strength is made perfect in weakness.
2 CORINTHIANS 12:9 NKJV

Sometimes, despite your best efforts, whether in a relationship, a business, a job, a school project, or whatever, your endeavor is not successful. Usually the failure doesn't come about because a person commits some sort of moral transgression. Instead, a person's skills are not matched to the task, or a business risk goes south, or someone's best efforts just aren't good enough.

As painful as these misadventures can be, a failure can be a rich opportunity for growth.

As you pick up the broken pieces and lay them before God in prayer, He can teach you some important lessons.

First, while you may fail, you are not a failure. You are a success because God's work in you makes you a success. Second, you can change the outcome next time. You can identify where things went awry and correct them. Or you can look for a different kind of challenge. Third, you may have lost the battle, but you will win the war. God will make sure of it.

God, use my mistakes to teach me about...

What's New Inside You?

Blessed are those who fear the Lord....
Their hearts are secure, they will have no fear.
PSALM 112:1, 8

God is ever interested in the condition of your heart. This is not the interest of a moral busybody; this is the interest of a loving friend who cares how you are feeling and what is going on inside.

What's new inside you? Your dreams, your disappointments, your schemes, your fears, your triumphs large and small—all of this matters to God. Prayer needs to be more than a list of requests or a formulaic checklist. It needs to be the deep sharing of two who truly love each other. When you let this kind of sharing be a part of your daily prayers, your relationship with God moves away from rote obedience to a deep friendship.

None of this excuses disobedience or cancels the moral distance between us and God. Rather it opens a new dimension of relationship and allows you to enjoy God almost as much as He enjoys you.

God, today my heart feels...

A Friend

There is a friend who sticks
closer than a brother.
PROVERBS 18:24 NKJV

Are you the type of person who makes friends easily? Or do you struggle to find and keep friends? Some people have a gift for forming friendships. They are like pied pipers who seem never to lack a throng of followers. But then there are those who find it difficult to have just one good friend, and some are altogether friendless.

Chalk it up to temperament, birth order, upbringing, or relational skills, some go through life very much alone. And, of course, many good people are shunned by others because they don't wear the right shoes or cut their hair the right way.

No matter where you fit on the friendship continuum, there's one person who is always open to receiving you as a friend: God. He is a friend to the friendless. He likes you, no matter how quirky your personality may be. He enjoys your company. If you're feeling isolated, if others have excluded you from their social circles, there is a friend who will never desert you. He's right here; as close as your prayers.

God, I love being Your friend because...

June 13

God's Heart

*I will give you a new heart
and put a new spirit in you.*
Ezekiel 36:26

The richest place in all the universe is the heart of God. Hidden inside God's heart are unlimited treasures of caring, compassion, patience, laughter, fun, righteous anger, unquenchable joy, kindness, courage, and contentment. When you pray, you are talking to the Person who experiences all of these things.

God's heart is like an ocean, limitless. Your own heart, by comparison, is like a thimble, limited. You can only experience a small part of God's heart at any one time. But if you ask God in prayer, He will share part of His heart with you. He might give you a deep compassion for someone you have never cared about before. Or He might allow you to taste His unquenchable joy. Your laughter and tears may come from a completely different place once you experience His heart.

Getting the gift of God's heart is the highest treasure anyone could receive. But be aware, it could change your life. With the gift of God's heart inside you, you will never look at anything the same way again.

God, having Your heart inside me would be...

Running Away from God

Strengthen the feeble hands, steady the knees that give way;
say to those with fearful hearts, "Be strong, do not fear."
ISAIAH 35:3–4

The most famous example of someone trying to run away from God is found in the biblical story of Jonah. Jonah was a man of God with a serious problem. He was prejudiced against a certain ethnic group. God saw this weakness as an opportunity. He sent Jonah to preach to that people group. And Jonah ran away.

There's one big problem with running away from God: Where can you go where He isn't? Jonah ran right into the arms of God. God used a violent storm to get him thrown off a boat and a great fish to transport him back to dry land. Try as he might, Jonah couldn't find a place where God wasn't.

We probably all have moments when we feel like running. This is when courage is needed to do the scary thing. This is when we need to turn around, face God squarely, and have a long, honest talk until we're both on the same page again.

God, I need to talk to You about...

....

....

....

....

....

....

....

Split-Second Prayer

We can be sure when we say,
"I will not be afraid because the Lord is my helper."
HEBREWS 13:6 NCV

Sometimes you don't have all day to pray. In fact, sometimes you have a second or less, where a silent, *Help!* is the best prayer you can pray. When that happens to you, don't worry. You're in good company.

One person whose life was changed by a split-second prayer was Nehemiah. Nehemiah was the cupbearer to a king. His job was to make sure the king's beverages weren't poisoned. It was also his job to look happy whether he felt happy or not.

This is where Nehemiah ran into a crisis. He was overwhelmed with sorrow and the king noticed. In that culture, that could mean death. But it was Nehemiah's split-second prayer that saved him. God gave him the courage and wisdom to propose a plan to the king for rebuilding the protective wall around the city of Jerusalem. The king heard the plan, liked it, and put Nehemiah in charge.

God, the split-second cry of my heart is...

Where Is God?

You came near when I called you, and you said, "Do not fear."
You, LORD, took up my case; you redeemed my life.
LAMENTATIONS 3:57–58

It's nice to know that God lives in the highest place, that nothing or no one can topple Him from His position as ruler of the universe. But, when you're in desperate need, it's also reassuring to know that God is near. God is equally in both places—enthroned as King of all, and right next to those who need Him.

The Bible makes it clear that God is with those who pray. He is sitting in the room with you, walking beside you, or riding in the car with you.

God is near those humble enough to acknowledge their need of Him.

When your life is falling apart, God is right there to put the pieces back together. The fact that He is with you shows that He cares. Because He is next to you, you know that He hears your prayers. He's close enough to hear the quietest whisper from your heart. With Him beside you, you know that you are protected from every evil.

God, I feel You close to me. I pray...

Mercy vs. Justice

Who is a God like you, who pardons sin and forgives the
transgression of the remnant of his inheritance?
You do not stay angry forever but delight to show mercy.
MICAH 7:18

As you pray, you can take comfort in knowing that God is both merciful and just. When a crime is committed, you can pray for both the victim and the perpetrator. God is just. He will not allow injustice to prevail. He will make things right. God is the author of criminal justice that protects the innocent and punishes the wrongdoer. God champions the victim and heals the hurting. Restitution is God's idea.

But God is also merciful. He longs to bring healing and transformation to both the injured party and the one who did wrong. God can and will forgive the worst of criminals, rebuilding their ruined lives, and transforming their hearts. As Jesus was dying on the cross, one of His last acts was to restore the robber who was being crucified next to Him.

Sooner or later, people you care about may find themselves on both sides of right and wrong. In either case, you can confidently pray for God's intervention. He will do what's right, offering both justice and mercy.

God, I need mercy for...

....

....

....

....

....

....

....

JUNE 18

Allowing the Supernatural

How great are your works, Lord, how profound your thoughts!
Psalm 92:5

Many times in the Bible, people asked God for a supernatural display of His power. Sometimes He granted their request. Sometimes He did not. For example, Herod eagerly desired to see Jesus perform some kind of miracle. But Jesus refused. God is supernatural. Doing the miraculous holds no difficulty for Him. But He is not here for our entertainment.

When you pray for a miracle, never place God in a position where He must act in order to protect His reputation. Rather, affirm His goodness and greatness regardless of how He responds to your prayer. Be sure that God's purposes are being served by your request. Open the door to the supernatural, but let God decide how He is going to act.

In the Bible, three young men were thrown into a fire for refusing to bow before a false god. They said, "Our God can deliver us, but even if He doesn't, we won't bow." By giving God the choice, they paved the way for a miracle.

God, open my heart to miracles so I can...

Coming to a Decision

Lord, tell me your ways. Show me how to live.
Guide me in your truth.
PSALM 25:4–5 NCV

Some decisions are not all that important. If you can't decide whether to buy the tan shirt or the blue shirt, flip a coin. But what should you do when decisions are important and you simply cannot get clear guidance?

Maybe you've searched the Bible, solicited the best advice you can get from the most reliable sources, and prayed earnestly, but the decision is still unclear. And now you've reached a deadline. What should you do?

The best thing to do when you don't know what to do is to do nothing. Suspend your decision for the time being. Stay where you are. Don't put that house on the market. Don't change jobs or get married. Wait.

When the time is right, God will give you the guidance you need. In the meantime, it's best to honor the last thing He told you to do. God is more than able to hand you the guidance you need. If He chooses to be silent, your response is to wait.

God, I will wait for Your guidance about...

June 20

Mountains and Valleys

*Elijah stepped forward and prayed... "Answer me, Lord,
answer me, so these people will know that you, Lord,
are God, and that you are turning their hearts back again."*
1 Kings 18:36–37

Elijah was a man of God who confronted an evil king with profound courage. He stood on a mountain challenging the proponents of a false religion with a simple test: "You prepare your sacrifice over there. I'll prepare mine over here. Let the true God consume the correct sacrifice with fire." Sure enough, fire fell; the true God was vindicated; a whole kingdom was in awe.

A week later, Elijah was running for his life, exhausted, depressed, and praying that he might die. Elijah's experience can mirror our own. We have mountaintop experiences with God, but then we descend into the valley of discouragement. When that happens, remember that God is just as real in the valley as He was on the mountain. You can still pray. Elijah prayed; but God did not repeat His mountaintop experience. Instead, He gave him a reassuring whisper that things were going to come together.

As you turn to God in moments of discouragement, you will be reassured too.

God, when I'm discouraged I will look to You for...

Many Approaches

Every good and perfect gift is from above, coming down from the
Father of the heavenly lights, who does not change like shifting shadows.
JAMES 1:17

In the Bible, we read the account of an invading army that sent a letter to a good king attempting to intimidate him by insulting the true God. The king took the offensive letter into God's temple and spread it out for God to read. The outcome was the defeat of the invading army.

There are literally thousands of ways to approach God in prayer. Are you naturally funny? God does indeed have a sense of humor.

Are you an artist? You may want to create a painting to present your heart to God. Or you may want to dance, or write a letter, or sing a song. The options are almost unlimited.

Prayer is just a bridge that brings you and God together. It can take any form you want. Be creative. Be original. Don't be afraid to try things. If they don't work, no problem; try something different. The key is to find the approach that works for you.

God, when I think about new ways to pray, I would like to try...

Salvaged by Prayer

[Love] always protects, always trusts, always hopes, always perseveres. Love never fails.
1 CORINTHIANS 13:7–8

King Manasseh was the worst of worst. He was an evil king who did almost everything wrong. He sacrificed his own children to false gods. He led an entire nation into false religion. He killed many innocent people. His list of crimes was nearly endless. When God judged it was time, He arranged an invasion; Manasseh was captured and led away in chains.

From his prison cell, Manasseh finally did something right. He apologized to God. He committed himself to following God for the rest of his life, no matter how short that might be. At the very end, his life was salvaged. He came home.

Many people may seem beyond the point of no return. But God is able to do the impossible. Every life is worth salvaging. God can still turn things around and bring beauty out of ashes. If God has put someone on your heart, keep on praying, even if that person keeps on straying. In the end, it may be your prayers that bring that person home.

God, when I think of people that need to come home I think of...

_____

_____

_____

_____

_____

_____

_____

_____

JUNE 23
Action and Prayer

Show me your faith without deeds, and I will show you my faith by my deeds.
JAMES 2:18

The thing about prayer is that it must go hand in hand with action. Too much action with not enough prayer and you'll be spinning your wheels. But prayer without action means missing opportunities to make a difference.

For example, you may want your children to love God. If you pray for them but never spend any time with them, then they lose all they could gain from your presence. But if you only spend time with them and neglect praying for them, then a whole supernatural dimension is missing.

This balance is borne out in the Bible. In a situation where God's people were threatened by hostile neighbors, the leaders prayed but they also posted a twenty-four-hour guard to protect against the threat. Both were necessary.

You know that you've achieved the right balance when you sense that your actions really are making a difference and your prayers really are breaking through. When in doubt, give the edge to prayer. God can do in a moment what would take you a lifetime.

God, actions that can be added to my prayers are...

Faith and Prayer

*Ye are all the children of God
by faith in Christ Jesus.*
GALATIANS 3:26 KJV

If you want answers to your prayers, the key is faith.

First, you must believe in God. Prayers to the universe or to no one in particular don't honor God. Prayer only has power when it is connected to the living God who responds when He is called upon simply because He has promised to do so.

Second, you must believe that God hears you. Over and over again, He tells us that He is listening when we speak. His ears are open to our prayers. He has given you access to His presence and the promise that He is waiting for you to come before Him.

Third, you must believe in God's goodness. He answers your prayers because He wants to—not because He has to. The source of His goodness is His love.

Finally, you must believe in God's timing. Parents don't always give their children what they want the moment they ask for it. God also has a timetable for your requests.

Don't waste your time praying in vain. Believe that God will do all that He says He will do.

God, let me honor You with my faith by...

The Ministry of Prayer

We constantly pray for you, that our God may make you worthy of his calling,
and that by his power he may bring to fruition your every desire
for goodness and your every deed prompted by faith.
2 THESSALONIANS 1:11

Some people are called by God into a ministry of prayer. Every believer should pray, but some people make prayer the main focus of their lives. These people are skilled at intercession and will happily spend hours each day before God. The apostles who started the early church were ministers of prayer. One early church leader spent so much time kneeling in prayer that he was said to have knees thickly calloused like a camel's.

If you sense that prayer is your ministry, then you are wise to learn all you can about it. You can begin by reading all the Bible has to say on the subject. And that's a lot. It would also be productive to connect with others who have a similar calling. Ask them deep questions and listen carefully to all they have to say. Be a good student of prayer but most of all—pray!

God, I believe my calling from You is...

June 26

Help in the Struggle

Who shall separate us from the love of Christ?
Shall tribulation, or distress, or persecution, or famine,
or nakedness, or peril, or sword?... Nay, in all these things
we are more than conquerors through him that loved us.
ROMANS 8:35, 37 KJV

All around the world, followers of God are engaged in pitched battles between good and evil. Some are confronting injustices. Others are persecuted for their faith. Still others are struggling to survive under extreme circumstances.

As a child of God, you have a deep connection with these brothers and sisters wherever they may be. You might never visit a field hospital in Sudan or a refugee camp in Colombia, but your prayers can be felt in all of these places. By your prayers, you enter prisons, hospitals, orphanages, and oppressed nations all over the world. By your prayers, you provide encouragement, comfort, and the strength to hold on to their beliefs.

The great apostle Paul asked people to join him in his struggle by praying for him. Modern-day Pauls all over the world depend on you for the same.

God, some of the struggles I'd like to pray for are...

A Reason for Thanks

The fruit of righteousness will be peace; its effect will be quietness and confidence forever.
ISAIAH 32:17

There are many reasons to give thanks to God—health, family, our relationship with Him, the gift of eternal life, friends, and opportunity—to name a few. But a foundational reason to thank God is this: He is righteous. In other words, He always does what is right and good because that's who He is.

If God were not righteous, then there would be no safety in the universe. Ultimately, no one could protect us from God Himself. At any moment, He could betray us, destroy us. But His righteousness allows us to live in safety. It allows us to trust Him It allows us to rest quietly in His love.

God will take everything that is wrong and eventually make it right. He simply could not do any less, for He will not allow evil to prevail. He is good and kind and most of all, righteous. Therefore, we can depend on Him to keep His promises.

Give thanks to God in your prayers for His perfect righteousness that covers and sustains us.

God, I want to thank You for...

JUNE 28

Proactive Prayer

Therefore, let everyone who is godly pray
to You in a time when You may be found;
surely in a flood of great waters they will not reach him.
PSALM 32:6 NASB

How would you feel about friends who come to you only when they need something from you? What if they ignored you most of the time, but when they were confronted with a time of crisis, they came running for help?

Clearly, that's no way to treat a friend. Friends invest in each other's lives because they want to. There are no strings attached. You take care of your friends and when you need them, they will be there for you.

Some people see no problem with praying to God only when they're in trouble. They acknowledge Him only when disaster strikes. But the Bible tells us that good people should pray to God while He may be found, so that they will be safe when the floods come in.

If things are going along smoothly for you, then this is the perfect time to build a relationship with God through prayer. Share your life. Express your gratitude. Laugh together. Plan together. Build a solid bond that will not be shaken when the ride gets rough.

God, I want more of You in my life because...

Entry Point

I will bless the LORD at all times;
His praise shall continually be in my mouth.
PSALM 34:1 KJV

There's something about giving thanks to God and offering praise that opens the door for a deeper relationship with Him and a more satisfying prayer life. As you focus on God's gifts and then on the character of the Giver of those gifts, your perspectives begin to change. Your problems shrink. Your faith grows. Your insight deepens.

No wonder then that the Bible offers this process as the best way to approach God. If you start with thanksgiving and add a healthy dose of praise, you enter into a more intimate place with God. Temptations lose their luster as you gain a better picture of who God is and what He offers to you because you realize that anything evil offers is only a cheap imitation of a much better gift from God.

If you get stuck when you're praying, giving thanks and offering praise is almost a guaranteed way to get unstuck. It gets you into the presence of God, and that's where the answers are.

God, I want to praise You for...

Full Circle

O LORD, I am your servant.... I will offer you a sacrifice of thanksgiving and call on the name of the LORD.
PSALM 116:16–17 NLT

It's difficult to fully measure the rewards of a life of prayer. In your journey with God, you will receive far more than just His answers, you will receive a relationship with Him that you wouldn't trade for anything. You will gain His heart of compassion, a place in His family, and the gift of knowing Him forever. As you walk with Him, you will be transformed. Others will be drawn to you, sensing the presence of God in your life. The purposes of evil that were directed toward your life will fall away. You may and probably will encounter storms and trials. But, in the end, you can smile and be at peace.

We start prayer with thanksgiving, and ultimately, that is where you come full circle. Your petitions have been heard, your prayers answered. God has given you more than you could have requested. And again you sink to your knees to give thanks.

Prayer is a gift that continues to give you peace, promise, hope, and courage. Open your heart and give Him thanks.

God, some of the rewards of prayer are...

JULY 1

It's Not in the Details

Pray in the Spirit on all occasions with all kinds of prayers and requests.
With this in mind, be alert and always keep on praying for all the Lord's people.
EPHESIANS 6:18

Next time you're out and about, take a good look around you. You likely don't know the names, much less the backgrounds, of the people you see. But you can be certain of one thing. Behind every smiling face are people with disappointments, hurts, doubts, and fears. Every one of them needs your prayers.

Near the end of his teaching about the armor of God, the apostle Paul emphasized the importance of Christians praying for other people, especially fellow believers in Jesus. Why? These prayers provide protection from the many influences that can undermine—or even destroy—a person's ability to believe and trust in the Lord.

Can you think of a person you can begin praying for every day? Perhaps you don't know all the details of that person's life, but God surely does. As you pray, you'll find your spirit emboldened by God's Spirit to pray with confidence, knowing that your words are a mighty weapon for good that will have a powerful impact on the heart and mind of someone you know.

Heavenly Father, the people I can begin praying for this week are...

God's Anxiety Antidote

Which of you by worrying can add one cubit to his stature?
MATTHEW 6:27 NKJV

Someone once said, "Worry is like a rocking chair: It gives you something to do, but it doesn't get you anywhere." Yet many of us just can't stop rocking. Anxiety disorders affect millions each year in the United States alone. It's a problem that impacts people from all walks of life.

Jesus Christ must have understood the way we worry. In the first sermon He preached He said, "Do not worry." Near the end of His ministry on earth, He told His disciples, "Don't let your hearts be troubled."

So what is God's antidote for what worries you today? Instead of focusing on what you can't do about the problem you're facing, choose instead, through prayer and worship, to focus on what God can do with that difficulty. Whether it's a struggle with your family, health, finances, or relationships, He can help you with it—and then give you His incomparable peace.

It's time to get off your rocker. Cast your cares on God, give Him your praise, and then be amazed as His comfort overwhelms you.

Lord, I want to pray and give You thanks today for...

The Times of Your Life

Though I walk in the midst of trouble, you preserve my life.
PSALM 138:7

Keeping a log of God's timely answers to your prayers is an uplifting practice. But what about the times when you don't see your prayers answered? What do you do when you find yourself feeling sad and disappointed? Should you record those times as well? Of course you should.

The Lord allows and even desires for you to declare such honest emotion. But He also loves when you trust Him. Even the prophet Jeremiah, often called the weeping prophet because of the despair he faced, cried out, "Great is Your faithfulness!" In his times of overwhelming sadness, he still knew the Lord was in control and would see him through to the end.

God will see you through as well. He has promised to stay by your side through joy and sorrow. He has promised never to leave you no matter what. Bring everything to Him and experience His joy, comfort, and faithfulness.

The difficulties I'm giving to You today, Lord, are...

....

....

....

....

....

....

....

....

Live Free in Him

Where the Spirit of the Lord is, there is freedom.
2 CORINTHIANS 3:17 NCV

Whether spoken by a Founding Father, a Civil War general, or a modern-day president, the link between physical freedom and the spiritual is undeniable. Thomas Jefferson said, "God who gave us life gave us liberty at the same time." Ulysses S. Grant encouraged people to look at the Bible "as the sheer anchor of your liberties; write its precepts on your heart and practice them in your lives." Ronald Reagan added that "Freedom is one of the deepest and noblest aspirations of the human spirit."

These three distinct generations of American leaders shared the same timeless message that rings true today for people in any country. An understanding of God and knowledge of His ways are not only central to a nation's liberty—but they're essential to the freedom of your heart and soul.

Decide to read the Bible daily and then pray about what you've learned, applying God's liberating truths to your life. It'll help you live free in Him, and declare your independence from the things that can bind your heart.

Lord God, help my life to be free of...

Air Supply

God is our protection and our strength.
He always helps in times of trouble.
PSALM 46:1 NCV

Recent years have seen many mining accidents, the most notorious happening in the nation of Chile. In most cases, rescuers dug a hole or a series of shafts through which the trapped miners could receive air and supplies. Sometimes this work proved to be the difference between life and death.

This is similar to the work of prayer, which drills a hole of life-sustaining faith through barriers of doubt and troublesome thoughts. Prayer can make all the difference for those trapped in difficult circumstances.

You have probably been on the receiving end of prayer at some point in your life as well. If so, you may have experienced the unexpected sense of inner peace and moments of clarity in the midst of confusion. You may have felt hope in the face of hopelessness. That's what prayer does.

Your prayers can be that air supply for those in trouble. You can be part of God's rescue team. It's a great privilege to work hand in hand with God, allowing Him to bring help, comfort, and blessing through you.

Father God, use my prayers to supply help to...

Morning Glory Rise

God's glory is on tour in the skies, God-craft on exhibit across the horizon.
PSALM 19:1 MSG

Have you ever risen early just to take in a sunrise? It's worth the effort to see the vivid shades of red, orange, and yellow ignite a backdrop of blue as the sun illuminates the clouds from behind its nightly hideaway.

God's glory is indeed wonderfully declared in nature. Yet His glory has even greater significance in our hearts and lives. The psalms declare that those who commit their way to the Lord and trust in Him will shine—going forward like the morning sun to be seen by all as a reflection of His life within them. If you have committed your way to Him, His glory is shining in you and blessing others.

Tomorrow morning, if possible, awake early. Catch the sunrise and meditate on the life-altering work of God that takes place daily in your heart and mind. Then with eyes wide open, offer a prayer to God, thanking Him for allowing His glory to be manifest in and through you. Thank Him for letting His sun rise in your heart.

God, help me display Your glory to someone today by...

JULY 7

Masterpiece in the Making

Put on the new self which is being renewed in knowledge in the image of its Creator.
COLOSSIANS 3:10

A sculptor once carved a magnificent lion out of a solid block of stone. When asked how he had accomplished such a marvelous masterpiece, he said, "It's easy. All I had to do was chip away everything that didn't look like a lion."

Each day, God whittles away those things in your life that aren't consistent with His character, transforming you into His image. He does this so that you will learn more about His ways and alter the way you think and react to what life brings your way each day. Your choices, your habits, and your values will more consistently reflect Him to everyone around you, as He helps you become what He wants you to be.

The Bible encourages you to take an active role in the sculpting of your life by choosing to change how you think—and He's provided direction to help you do just that. Approach Him confidently in prayer and ask Him to chip away at you and reveal the beautiful masterpiece inside.

Lord God, three things I can do this week to change my attitude are...

....

....

....

....

....

....

....

JULY 8

What Is That Tree?

When you are tempted, he will also provide
a way out so that you can endure it.
1 CORINTHIANS 10:13

Adam and Eve had it made in the shade. They lived in a beautiful garden created just for them. They could go wherever they wanted and eat whatever pleased them—except for the fruit of one specific tree. Yet it was that one tree, the promise that went with it, and the deceptive twist their enemy put on it that ended their stay in the garden.

It's amazing how the things we shouldn't do are the very things that seem most attractive. But the essence of the freedom God offers is that we now have the ability through Him to make good decisions and avoid those things that aren't best for us. All we have to do is ask for His help.

What's that one tree in your life? Whether it's an action, an attitude, or even an addiction, God can help you cut it down as you spend time with Him. Humble yourself before Him in prayer, and ask Him to help you make eternally healthy choices.

Lord God, help me make good choices about...

Good Returns

*Give thanks in all circumstances; for this is
the will of God in Christ Jesus for you.*
1 THESSALONIANS 5:18 NRSV

No matter how much we try, we can't control the circumstances that'll come our way. We can, however, control our outlook.

Why? For one thing, we never know when those unexpected circumstances might lead to great things. Christopher Columbus, searching for a direct route to Asia, stumbled onto the Americas. Thomas Edison invented a phonograph while attempting to perfect the telegraph and telephone. When Benjamin Franklin experienced electricity while flying a kite during a storm, he invented the lightning rod.

The Bible encourages us to have an optimistic outlook, particularly when it comes to serving God. Jesus said, "Give, and it will be given to you." As we're faithful to Him with our time, talents, and possessions, the Lord promises that we'll receive from Him in return all that we need.

Will you pray today with optimism, giving your doubts and fears to Him? Doing so will open up your possibilities and give you the assurance that no matter what your day brings, God will be there to help you make the best of it.

Father, help me up my optimism concerning...

The First

After Jesus rose from the dead early on Sunday morning,
the first person who saw him was Mary Magdalene.
MARK 16:9 NLT

There's just something wonderfully memorable about the first time you experience something, isn't there? Your first car. Your first date. Your very first kiss. Those experiences are permanently embedded in your mind, for better or for worse.

Yet someone in the Bible had a first that beats all others. Three days after watching Jesus die, Mary Magdalene, one of His closest followers, stood outside the tomb weeping. She couldn't believe her eyes. His body was gone, and she had no idea where it was! Suddenly a man she presumed to be the gardener asked her why she was crying and gently called her by name. As He spoke, Mary realized who He was—Jesus! She quickly went to tell His disciples the incredible news. She was the first person to see Jesus alive after His resurrection.

Perhaps you're going through something for the very first time that you find hard to believe. Call upon Jesus in prayer and tell Him what's going on in your heart. He'll tenderly guide you and restore your faith in Him.

Lord, this is the first time I've had to deal with...

Reveal Your Treasure

How precious is your steadfast love, O God!
All people may take refuge in the shadow of your wings.
PSALM 36:7 NRSV

Our homes are adorned with common vases, jars, and other knick-knacks that are generally used solely for decoration. But in ancient eras, such containers sometimes had a more covert function: concealing treasure. Because they didn't attract attention to themselves, their costly contents often went undetected. Roman conquerors would even melt down precious metals looted from vanquished foes and pour them into clay pots so the booty could remain safely hidden.

God has chosen to place the incredible treasure of His love inside the common vessels of frail, flawed, vulnerable human beings. Why? So that when we reveal His love to others through an act of kindness or by praying for them, it's undeniable that His power, not our own, is at work. His strength and sufficiency is made evident through our weakness and insufficiency.

Today, break open your jar of clay and let the treasure of His love pour out. Allow your prayers to flow for others. They'll richly benefit from the wealth of God's hope stored in you.

Father, help me reveal Your love for others through...

Take the Plunge

*When you call upon me and come
and pray to me, I will hear you.*
JEREMIAH 29:12 NRSV

A famous photo published decades ago in *Life* magazine shows an overhead view of three teenage boys jumping from a high cypress branch toward a pond below. One boy looks terrified, plummeting feet first, his arms flapping. Another boy goes toward the water head first, arms ramrod stiff, like he just wants the experience to end. But the third boy stands out. He's floating, his body in a relaxed arch, arms hanging in an upside-down V. He appears daring but poised.

When we're ready to dive into the realm of prayer, asking God to respond to our needs while interceding on behalf of others, it can be downright scary. Fears and doubts want to hold us back. Yet as we take the plunge, we can do so with confidence that God promises to hear us and respond according to His good and perfect will.

Remember, the pressure's not on you to answer your prayers. You simply need to relax and ask, then trust in Him. He'll take care of the rest.

God, the hindrances that seem be affecting my prayer life are...

From the Mouths of Babes

Jesus said, "Let the little children come to Me,
and do not forbid them;
for of such is the kingdom of heaven."
MATTHEW 19:14 NKJV

"Now I lay me down to sleep. I pray the Lord my soul to keep."

Did you ever pray those words, or something like them, as a child? Whatever you said, you almost certainly associate that memory with a feeling of security or rest, especially if a parent or some other trusted adult was praying with you.

Yet how often do we actually pray with the children in our lives today? Whether you're a parent, grandparent, or have some other role in the life of a child, it's obviously good to pray for them. But it's infinitely better if you can literally pray *with* them, letting your presence and your words support their act of faith to trust God with their prayers.

You'll get excited, and your faith will blossom as you watch these children discover that prayer is not only a way to communicate with God, but one that you believe in enough to practice with them.

Lord God, help me pray with the children in my life about...

....

....

....

....

....

....

....

Making Thankfulness Routine

Give thanks to the Lord, for he is good; his love endures forever.
1 CHRONICLES 16:34

You've probably heard the classic song lyrics, "Accentuate the positive...eliminate the negative." It's a catchy tune—but how can its simple principle catch on in terms of how we look at God and our prayer lives?

A great place to start is to establish a regular routine that involves reading the Bible, praying individually, and praying with a spouse, family member, or close friend. Then you will want to use those times to focus and meditate on the goodness of God. If you can't keep up this routine, that's okay. Begin with just a few times a week and slowly build from there. The point is to offset the stress and negativity that often comes your way with the attitude of gratitude that your new routine will create.

Simply put, be thankful. Think about the positive things that occur in your life: good health, a place to live, for example. Give each to God in prayer. Then make an ongoing "Praises and Blessings" list and review it often. It'll accentuate your life!

Heavenly Father, four things that I can be grateful for today are...

JULY 15

Overcoming the Obstacles

I press on to take hold of that for which
Christ Jesus took hold of me.
PHILIPPIANS 3:12

Have you ever started something you fully meant to finish—only to never get it done? If so, what happened to stop you? You probably ran into some form of opposition, and opposition, sadly, is part of life.

Sometimes opposition comes in the form of a circumstance that detours us, such as divorce, job loss, or financial challenges. Other times, it can be a self-made excuse, such as fear, criticism, age, or perfectionism.

How do we overcome these setbacks and start anew? The apostle Paul tells us in the Bible:

Forget what lies behind. Strain forward to what lies ahead. Press on toward the goal. We are meant to finish the race. But we also need to remember that there's no victory in life without a chance of losing. It's that unknown, along with opposition, that often brings us the greatest opportunities to grow.

Whatever has kept you from a more intimate relationship with God in the past, leave it behind and press on! Seek Him—and experience His presence as never before.

Father, the obstacles that have hindered my prayer life in the past are...

A Beautiful Metamorphosis

I will listen to what God the LORD says;
he promises peace to his people, his faithful servants.
PSALM 85:8

The metamorphosis of a caterpillar into a butterfly is truly astounding. It can take anywhere from one week to a year depending on the species, but wouldn't that be an incredible process to watch? During the pupal stage, the tissues and organs of the caterpillar actually melt away, only to miraculously reassemble themselves into that of an adult butterfly. The result is a profoundly beautiful insect that flutters off to repeat the unique creative process.

We're also undergoing a metamorphosis, but it's one that's never-ending. God is gradually transforming us into His likeness. This is done as He literally takes what already belongs to Him—His strength and wisdom, the very essence of who He is—and makes it known to us. The main way God does this is through prayer. As we ask and He speaks, He gives us insight, direction and help; that is, as long as we're listening.

Try to listen more attentively the next time you pray. Whatever changes within you as a result is sure to be a beautiful sight.

Lord, as I prayed today, I heard You tell me...

JULY 17

Seeking True Success

Remember the LORD in all you do,
and he will give you success.
PROVERBS 3:6 NCV

Just watch the people around you for any time at all, and you'll find it to be true: Just because someone is successful doesn't mean he or she is truly a success.

You likely know many people who seem incredibly organized and have it all together. And yet you know they live daily with tremendous, unhealthy levels of stress. They've sacrificed family relationships for work. They're unhappy and harried. Perhaps these people are friends or family members. Perhaps this even describes you.

The difference between being successful and being a true success begins with what's in the heart. It's not about planning or compiling a to-do list on your own. It starts with a meaningful conversation with God about what He wants *on* that list—about what He wants to accomplish, and who He wants you to be.

Today, begin seeking the Lord. Intercede for those you see mired in their own successfulness. And pray for yourself, that God would reveal His will for your life and help you become His true success story.

God, I rededicate what's in my heart to You by...

Step Beyond the Excuses

For the Spirit God gave us does not make us timid,
but gives us power, love and self-discipline.
2 TIMOTHY 1:7

It's so easy to make excuses to keep from doing something you know you need to do, isn't it? You might be thinking: *I don't have the right background or experience. I'm too set in my ways to be making changes in my life. Who am I to be taking this on? People won't accept me. People won't listen to me. Others are much more qualified.*

If any of those excuses sound comforting, you're in good company. They are the precise excuses used by Moses in response to God's call.

You know—Moses who led the great Exodus, parted the Red Sea, defeated the Egyptians.

Look at what Moses accomplished when he stepped beyond the excuses and into the flow of God's power and sustenance. His life impacted a nation and still influences lives today. Now, imagine what you can do in prayer to benefit yourself, your loved ones, and even the world at large when you move past your excuses?

Lord, help me overcome my excuses for not having a consistent prayer life, like...

Start by Stopping

Get wisdom, and whatever else you get, get insight.
PROVERBS 4:7 NRSV

You've undoubtedly noticed there are two kinds of people—those who are slow to rise, and those who are up before the first break of dawn. Often, they end up married to each other, resulting in some interesting dynamics in the home.

Most morning people want to get started early on the day's task list. No slowing down, no need for delay. It's just, "Go!" And yet when they hit the ground running, they sometimes end up on the ground. Why? Perhaps it's because they didn't take enough time to get their bearings. They might have done better to begin their day by *thinking* first, not doing. The will to succeed is worthless if there is not first the will to prepare.

Start by stopping—stopping to think about what God wants from you today and taking just a few minutes to gain insight from Him in prayer. This is an important step that will result in a life that pleases God and impacts others. And isn't that what really matters?

Father, after I rise, remind me to take five minutes to pray for…

Step into the Wind

I have set the LORD always before me: because he is at my right hand, I shall not be moved.
PSALM 16:8 KJV

Let's say you start doing something new and positive—eating better, exercising more, or increasing the time you spend with God in prayer—only to have someone throw an obstacle in your way. That someone may be a spouse who doesn't understand your commitment or friends who feel your new challenge will give you less time together. Or maybe you can relate to the classic "Pogo" comic strip by cartoonist Walt Kelly: "We have met the enemy, and he is us."

How do you respond to those who throw obstacles in your way? Do you give in or lean forward into the new, improved phase of life God has for you? It's like when you're walking against a stiff wind: you just put your head down and step into it, determined to arrive at your destination.

When you're doing something right, don't be deterred by what others say or think. Pray for those who oppose you, then keep going. You'll get there.

Father, my prayer for those who throw obstacles in my way is...

Don't Snooze on God

Whether you turn to the right or to the left, your ears
will hear a voice behind you saying, "This is the way; walk in it."
ISAIAH 30:21

The alarm clock is a unique contraption. Once you become accustomed to it waking you consistently, your mind can actually condition itself to awaken mere moments before the alarm sounds. You're ready to turn it off seconds after it comes on! But ignore that same alarm for a few days straight and, before you know it, you're sleeping through it as though it doesn't even exist.

It's kind of the same with God. If you consistently set aside His guidance as He gently speaks words of counsel or conviction to you in prayer, you'll eventually stop hearing Him altogether. Yet when you attune your mind to daily recognize and pay attention to the direction He gives you when you pray, not only will you hear Him but you will also begin to anticipate His instruction, responding even before you hear Him say it.

Don't hit the snooze button when God speaks. Train your spiritual ear by praying, listening, and then obeying Him consistently.

Father, I will train myself to listen when You speak by...

Where Great Advice Begins

*Let the wise also hear and gain in learning,
and the discerning acquire skill.*
PROVERBS 1:5 NRSV

In his book *How I Pray*, Billy Graham told the story of a young company president who'd instructed his secretary not to have him disturbed because of an important appointment he had every morning in his office.

One day the chairman of the board came by, insisting to see the president. Despite the secretary's objections, the chairman walked past her and opened the office door. There he saw the president of his corporation beside his desk, kneeling in prayer. The chairman softly closed the door. "Is this usual?" he asked the secretary.

She said, "Yes, he does this every morning." The chairman responded, "No wonder I come to him for advice."

You're not the only beneficiary of a consistent personal prayer life. As you prioritize your time spent with God, you'll be given renewed strength, deeper peace, and greater wisdom not only for yourself but also for others. So create and maintain a daily practice of prayer, whether it's at your office desk or beside the living room sofa.

Lord, I believe a consistent prayer life is important because...

....

....

....

....

....

....

....

JULY 23

Prayer Power Unleashed

"Not by might nor by power, but by my Spirit,"
says the LORD *Almighty.*
ZECHARIAH 4:6

Some people relegate prayer to a last resort, to be attempted only when nothing else is working. Others use prayer as a crutch to make them feel better. But prayer can and should be so much more than that in our lives.

When the apostle James chose to write about prayer in the Bible, he used the prophet Elijah as an illustration of powerful, effective prayer. He told how Elijah's intercessions in a time of severe drought ultimately brought desperately needed rain and new, life-saving crops. Many lives were undoubtedly spared through the answer to Elijah's fervent prayers. They were both powerful and effective because Elijah was in regular communication with God. He prayed for God's purposes to be accomplished, not his own. And he never gave up.

When you decide to make prayer a daily, dynamic part of your life, it will change you—and others will be impacted as well. Make prayer the foundation of your relationship with God and the conduit through which His mighty power and purpose is unleashed.

Lord, I trust You to do amazing things through my prayers like...

Lunch-Break Intercessions

Walk worthy of the Lord unto all pleasing,
being fruitful in every good work,
and increasing in the knowledge of God.
COLOSSIANS 1:10 KJV

Ever wondered how to incorporate prayer into a daily routine at work? It's possible, even when your place of employment isn't a ministry or a church.

One woman who worked as a receptionist in a busy office did it this way. On her lunch break, she'd pull from her purse a list of military men and women she had committed to pray for— and right there, while she ate, she interceded silently for them. She prayed for them by name, and asked God to keep them safe as they served our nation in war zones around the world. As a result, she felt closer to God and experienced less stress as she dealt with customers because her attitude toward them was more loving and less negative.

No matter what you do for a living, take God to work with you. Ask Him to show you how you can find a place for prayer for yourself and others. It'll improve your prayer life and change your overall perspective for the better.

Father, some ideas I have for praying at work are...

Making Room for God

Seek those things which are above, where Christ is, sitting at the right hand of God.
Set your mind on things above, not on things on the earth.
COLOSSIANS 3:1–2 NKJV

You've probably heard it said that time is something you never have enough of, but there's always time for the things you prioritize. You automatically go to your job, or school, or do household chores such as preparing meals, and why is that? Because you have to, right? Same goes for sleeping. These are all necessary for daily living, even survival.

Making time for the things you *don't* have to do is where you need to make a decision, and all too often other options are given far more time than, say, reading the Bible or talking to God in prayer.

Make a list of all the things that aren't necessary for daily living but that you choose to do anyway. Is there just one item you can decrease, or set aside altogether, to make room for God? As you follow through, you'll grow wonderfully closer to Him.

Lord, some of the priorities I believe I can replace with prayer are...

The Name Says It All

*Jesus said, "I tell you, everyone who acknowledges
me before others, the Son of Man also will
acknowledge before the angels of God."*
LUKE 12:8 NRSV

What's in a name? Apparently an awful lot for some of the rich and famous. We'd never recognize the talents of Charles Carter, Eugene Orowitz and Jerome Levitch unless we knew their stage names. They are Charlton Heston, Michael Landon, and Jerry Lewis. Others with normal names select an unusual moniker, such as Caryn Johnson (better known as Whoopi Goldberg). For these celebrities, how they've identified themselves determines our perception of them.

"Son of Man" was Jesus' preferred title for Himself, used more than seventy times in the New Testament and never by anyone else but Him. It identified Him as the one perfect man who, on behalf of all mankind, would destroy the power of death and bring eternal life to all who would accept Him.

You undoubtedly know someone who needs the Son of Man as Savior. Pray for that person over the next week, and ask God to give you a greater perception of who Christ is in your own life.

God, help me draw closer to You as I pray for...

Rest of Our Being

Blessed be the Lord, who daily loads us with benefits, the God of our salvation!
PSALM 68:19 NKJV

Call it the dynamic trio—three wonderful benefits that you'll enjoy as you dedicate more time and attention to developing your prayer life.

Prayer, first, allows you to take the load off yourself. How? You must exercise faith to pray, and when you do, you give up your burdens to God. Next, you develop a sense of discipline that carries over to other areas. You'll find you have increased ability and willpower to establish other good habits such as consistent exercise, healthy eating, or more productive work practices.

Finally, prayer builds the spiritual community in your home. It gives you and your loved ones an increased realization that you are one as a family and serve the same God.

As a human being, you were created as a physical, mental, and spiritual entity. When you pray regularly, you're stimulating the spiritual part of your being that all too often lies dormant. This makes you whole, more complete in Him, and better able to love God and serve Him with all the rest of your being.

Heavenly Father, I can give more time and effort to my prayer life by...

Pursuits in Order

To every thing there is a season, and a time to every purpose under the heaven.
ECCLESIASTES 3:1 KJV

It's easy to take time for leisure and entertainment, isn't it? These activities feel good and have a payoff that is immediately apparent. They're fun, and we look forward to them, but they may not be that wise.

Solomon, the writer of one of the Bible's most underrated books, Ecclesiastes, understood that there is a time for everything, and a season for every activity. After a life filled with pursuits and all their payoffs, the man who had gained everything knew that only one pursuit was truly important: the acquisition of God's wisdom.

No, it's not easy to make appropriate time for pursuits that may not feel good at first, but they will have a far greater payoff: pursuits such as seeking God through daily devotions or just being quiet and listening for His voice in prayer. As you begin to purposefully and consistently do these things, you'll not only discover it's time well spent, but you'll find yourself more fulfilled—and all the wiser.

Father, to increase my prayer time, help me decrease other activities, like...

Watch Your Blind Spots

*It was by faith that Noah heard God's warnings
about things he could not yet see.*
HEBREWS 11:7 NCV

Before becoming president, Ronald Reagan was a popular actor married to Hollywood star Jane Wyman. One day he came home and was shocked to learn his wife was divorcing him. "I suppose there had been warning signs," he wrote in his memoir, "if only I hadn't been so busy."

Warning signs in your personal life are just like the blind spot when you're driving your car. You must be aware of those things lurking outside your line of sight that could knock you off course, even bring total destruction. Your blind spot could be almost anything: Ignoring the wise advice of a spouse or trusted colleague. Frittering away time on social networking sites. Bringing work stress home in the form of anger and criticism.

Prayer will give you better vision in your relationships. As you consistently bring your most intimate needs and concerns to God, He'll enable you to see potential trouble before you end up in a total wreck. Don't disregard the warning signs. Seek God, hear His counsel, and act on His direction.

Today, God, I ask for your guidance in my relationships with...

_____

_____

_____

_____

_____

_____

_____

Color Your Life

You show me the path of life.
In your presence there is fullness of joy;
in your right hand are pleasures forevermore.
PSALM 16:11 NRSV

Many people spend each day merely surviving in their relationships and spiritual life. They go through the motions, waving goodbye as they leave for work, making dinner plans, going to kids' activities. But they've lost a deeper connection. There could be more, but it just seems too much of an effort to try.

If you or someone you know is in survival mode, it's time to take a bold step toward a greater quality of life. It might be uncomfortable at first, but true contentment is hard to find in mediocrity. Prayer is a great place to start. Praying alone, or with your spouse or children, will help you cut through the murky routine of simply getting through life and take you to the deeper, more significant, more fulfilling areas of your personal life and your relationships.

As you listen and learn about these areas and then give them to God, asking for His purposes to be accomplished, life will take on new color. It'll become vibrant, renewed, and anything but mediocre.

God, I will courageously move from survival to fulfillment by...

Living in Victory

Be of good courage, and he shall strengthen your heart, all ye that hope in the LORD.
PSALM 31:24 KJV

He was all growl but no bite, lacking vim or verve. He boasted, "I'll fight you with one paw tied behind my back," yet the Cowardly Lion sobbed miserably when Dorothy slapped him for chasing Toto. "You're nothing but a great big coward!" she said as the so-called King of the Forest wiped away tears with his tail.

Unlike the movie *The Wizard of Oz*, there are no cowardly lions in the Bible, which uses the word "lion" to describe both Christ and the devil. The latter is called a roaring, devouring lion that seeks to destroy you, even your very relationship with God. But the "Lion of Judah," which the Bible identifies as Jesus, is a mighty champion who not only vanquished the power death had over you, but strengthens you daily to live in victory through Him.

So the next time you feel overwhelmed or afraid, know that Christ will fight the battle with you and give you all the courage you need, as you give your fears and concerns to Him in prayer. There's nothing cowardly about that.

Lord God, as I pray today, I feel worried or fearful about...

....

....

....

....

....

....

....

Hurry Up and Be Patient

You will be strengthened with all his
glorious power so you will have all
the endurance and patience you need.
COLOSSIANS 1:11 NLT

In a world where everything is rush, rush, rush, patience is often a difficult thing to practice. What do you do when you have to wait? Lash out at others even though it's not their fault? Wait passively for the situation to change, feeling helpless and out of control?

No matter what the situation, there are times when having patience, though temporarily annoying, can be a positive milestone. It can give you the time to prioritize the steps needed to be fully prepared, assess where you are in the process or, most importantly, take the circumstance to God in prayer.

As you slow down enough to seek His guidance for whatever it is that's making you wait or holding you back, an amazing thing will happen. You'll be given renewed perspective for the situation, and as this occurs, you'll discover that waiting patiently is not only a good thing, but something you'll start doing more often. It'll lessen your anxiety, bring peace of mind, and help you discern God's purposes for your life.

Enable me, God, to be patient concerning...

The Will to Forgive

If you forgive others their trespasses, your heavenly Father will also forgive you.
MATTHEW 6:14 NRSV

When we pray, perhaps the most challenging thing we have to do is forgive someone who has wronged us. It's also the most essential.

Corrie ten Boom, who survived a Nazi concentration camp but watched helplessly as her sister withered away and died an excruciating death, had a remarkable encounter following World War II. Visiting a church in Munich, she was approached by a former camp guard who had become a Christian. He came to ask Corrie for forgiveness. She didn't want to do it, but

Corrie grasped the guard's hand and told him she forgave him. She later said she had never known God's love so intensely as she did at that moment.

Giving forgiveness in prayer is an act of your will, but Jesus was clear in the Bible that the choice to forgive others is not optional. Yet it is also the greatest way to declare God's love to another person, and it will bring you both unexpected peace for your minds and cleansing healing for your hearts when you do.

Lord God, help me forgive...

Defy the Deceptions

Give yourselves completely to God. Stand against the devil, and the devil will run from you. Come near to God, and God will come near to you.

JAMES 4:7–8 NCV

If you've ever taken a foreign language class, you know that feeling of linguistic despair. It comes when someone expert in that language visits to test your ability to carry on a conversation. Just when you thought you'd mastered your new tongue, his fluency and rapidity of speech leaves you, quite literally, at a loss for words.

You should have no such trouble, however, when the devil talks to you. Lies are his native language, and he's very proficient with their use. Look up every Bible verse referring to the devil. You'll discover that, among other things, he turns people's hearts to do wrong and even snatches truth away from those who hear it.

Every day, you will hear his lies. But as you faithfully pray, God will teach you to recognize those lies and take a stand against them. He'll also help you speak the truth of God's Word and defy the devil's deceptions. You'll never again find yourself at a loss for words spiritually.

Heavenly Father, I've heard lies that I almost believed, like...

....

....

....

....

....

....

....

....

Anticipate the Amazing

If you can believe, all things are possible to him who believes.
MARK 9:23 NKJV

Imagine that you were there the day Jesus ascended into heaven after His resurrection. The one without whom you would feel lost in life was suddenly leaving! But before He departed, He said: "Go—and make disciples. But first, wait in Jerusalem for a gift from my Father."

When you're expecting something big, something you've never seen before, to arrive, what do you do? You try to stay focused. You pray. More than that, you pray together, with people of the same mind and passion. And for Jesus' followers, it wasn't long before the incredible happened, and the early church was born.

Are you still waiting for an answer, perhaps even a miraculous one, to your prayers for someone you care about? Perhaps it's more personal, and you're wrestling with taking a personal leap of faith. Whatever the case, don't take your focus off God. Pray expectantly, and with others, remaining sensitive to hear what He has to say and anticipating something amazing from Him.

God, I will believe You today for big answers to prayers for...

He'll Hear Your Urgent Call

Let all who are faithful offer prayer to you; at a time of distress,
the rush of mighty waters shall not reach them.
PSALM 32:6 NRSV

For ships at sea, it is dot-dot-dot, dash-dash-dash, dot-dot-dot—SOS. In the air, the call is "Mayday!" Worldwide these communications are understood to mean distress—help urgently needed.

Fortunately, God has provided a distress communication. He says, "Pray." It's our mainline to reach God and express our true feelings and needs. Throughout the Psalms, David used this mainline often and effectively. Over his life, he experienced the treachery of a close friend, personal failure hurting those he loved, and threats at every turn. The burdens were too heavy to carry alone. So David cried out, sometimes around the clock, with all the honesty he could muster—and his God heard him.

In the maydays of life, don't tap on the Morse Code keys or yell into the radio. Call on God in prayer, certain that He will hear you. Then dedicate that same passion to interceding for the turmoil and dangers facing those you love and hold dear, unwavering in your belief that your prayers will be heard.

Today, God, I ask You to help these people who are experiencing distress...

An Ageless Pursuit

You will call upon me and come and pray to me,
and I will listen to you. You will seek me and find me
when you seek me with all your heart.
JEREMIAH 29:12–13

The average lifespan in the Classical Greek and Roman periods was a mere twenty-eight years. Yet in the New Testament we meet the prophetess Anna who, at the ripe old age of eighty-four, had lived three times longer than average.

So what had she deemed important during her life? The Bible says Anna spent her days in worship and prayer. Can you imagine the wisdom she had gleaned over her years; the closeness she had with God? Her strongest desire was to see the Messiah for herself— and when she finally did, she did not contain her enthusiasm.

Whether you are twenty-seven or seventy-seven, you are neither too young nor too old to make knowing God your strongest desire. Watch for Him and His working power in your life, and keep praising and interceding in the meantime. Pursue God diligently for yourself and for the urgent needs of your friends and loved ones. There's no better and more life-impacting way to spend your days.

God, I would like to praise You for...

To the Heights

*We have troubles all around us, but we
are not defeated. We do not know what to do,
but we do not give up the hope of living.*
2 CORINTHIANS 4:8 NCV

The poster in the human resources office showed a three-branched seedling at the base of a giant sequoia. The caption on the poster read "Determination." Webster's Dictionary defines determination as "the act of deciding definitely and firmly."

Living with faith in God is so much more than feeling. It takes determination. Sure, some aspects are easier than others. But to have faith in the face of, say, a cancer diagnosis is one thing; to be joyful in that same circumstance is quite another. Yet as you consistently spend time in prayer—either for yourself or on behalf of someone else who is afflicted—your faith is energized and you understand that God remains in control, no matter how much things seem to be in chaos.

Help your faith grow from a little sapling to the heights of a giant sequoia tree by prioritizing your relationship with God. Make your determined, firm decision now to establish faith-filled prayer in your life, in good times or bad.

God, I give You the difficult trials I'm facing today, especially...

Out of the Dark

I am the light of the world. Whoever follows me will never walk in darkness, but will have the light of life.
JOHN 8:12

"It dawned on me." "The fog lifted and I finally understood." "Let's shed some light on the subject." You've probably used these phrases to describe what happened when you gained a specific insight or discerned a previously hidden truth. Maybe you've wanted a light bulb to be turned on in your mind and spirit because you felt in the dark about something unexpected or difficult in your life.

God created light. First He created physical light and then He created inner light to help you understand who He is, who you are, and what He wants from you. His desire is to shed light on your confusion and help you understand what you can do about the circumstances you're facing. As you pray, rest assured that God will give you the direction you need. And, the wisdom you'll receive will give you a feeling of peace and security that will brighten your outlook and energize your faith.

Today, ask God for insight and seek the light only He can give.

God, I need Your guidance today for...

....

....

....

....

....

....

....

Getting God's Attention

*The eyes of the Lord are on the righteous and
his ears are attentive to their prayer.*
1 PETER 3:12

Have you ever said, "Eyes, please!" when you've wanted a child to pay attention to you? You're emphasizing the need to look first so you can be sure the child is hearing what you're saying.

In the Psalms, David often asked God to turn His eyes and ears to him. Because of the pressure he felt, either from the criticisms of others or the trouble he saw in the world around him, David needed reassurance from God that his prayers would be heard and answered.

Can you relate to that? Troubles abound, and the world can be a negative place. But by reaching out to God in prayer, you can find confidence and assurance that God is paying attention and He cares. His eyes are trained on you and His ears are open to your pleas.

David trusted that God was listening and He was not disappointed. God saw and heard and took care of those things that concerned him. God will take care of you in the same way.

Give me Your help today, God, for the difficulties of...

How Are You Wired?

The LORD is near to all who call on him, to all who call on him in truth.
PSALM 145:18

How do you respond in times of need or great distress? Perhaps you get angry and yell, or quietly go off by yourself and sulk. Or maybe you find it best to go straight to bed and let yourself slip into the numbing solace of unconsciousness.

When under duress, the Bible records that King David often cried out to God in frustration. In contrast, the apostle Peter on one occasion was jailed and bound in chains, yet he slept so soundly an angel had to awaken him.

When disturbing circumstances take place, it's wonderful to have the faith of Peter and simply rest. But you may not be able to do that. God knows how you are wired—and accepts you regardless.

Let this comfort and cheer you today. You can come into God's presence at any time, and in any way, through your prayers. Loud or quiet, agitated or calm, God will hear your pleas for help. Come to Him confidently. He will answer and give you peace.

Today, God, I need Your comfort to help me through...

A Way into Wisdom

If any of you is lacking in wisdom, ask God,
who gives to all generously and ungrudgingly,
and it will be given you.
JAMES 1:5 NRSV

What is one of the most important things to pray for when you are going through a trial or temptation? Strength? Deliverance? How about wisdom?

When you endure challenges, godly knowledge will help you make the most of the opportunities God gives you to mature in the midst of the circumstance. Wisdom will help you apply the knowledge gained through the experience for your good and His glory. The Bible gives insight on *how* to ask for His wisdom, and it's quite encouraging. In the book of James, it says to ask in faith, knowing that God is anxious to answer, and He will never scold you. Finally, you're exhorted to believe and not doubt.

Whatever it is you're dealing with today, don't ask first for a way out. Pray for a way into His wisdom, and then use the discernment He provides to move through the trial—and on toward what He has next for you. Remain bold and optimistic, understanding that God is ordering your every step.

Lord God, I ask for wisdom about...

August 12
Finding Your True Devotion

Let the hearts of those who seek the Lord rejoice. Look to the Lord and his strength; seek his face always.
Psalm 105:3–4

In today's hustle-bustle society, there's no end to the demands on our lives. Be it our careers, our families, the things we enjoy for leisure, or a combination of all of these and more, the different aspects of our lives are always vying for our time and devotion.

To what or whom are you fully committed? Do you dedicate your efforts to your job or a favorite television show, or work fervently to champion the cause of a favorite organization? Or, can you say that you spend a great deal of your energy devoted to seeking God? In other words, what are you truly devoted to?

Devoting yourself to your relationship with God has great rewards and benefits. Your life will take on new meaning and purpose as you read the Bible, meditate on its truths, and approach God with confidence in prayer. Intercede for your needs and pray for others that they, too, will be devoted to knowing God better.

Help me, God, to be more devoted to seeking You by...

Jumping for Joy

[A] person can pray to God and find favor with him, they will see God's face and shout for joy.
JOB 33:26

Do you jump for joy? Unless you're naturally overexuberant (or, perhaps, a sports fan), you probably don't often let your feet leave the ground in a burst of happiness. This is because, generally, your circumstances don't call for such a reaction. Real life, even in cheery moments, is a tad more mundane.

That's what makes the Bible so relevant. It provides basic instruction that you can apply to your everyday existence. When it says to be joyful always with prayer and thanksgiving, God is giving you a way to navigate whatever circumstances come your way. He is suggesting that you, at various times throughout each day, come to Him with a thankful heart because you know He will work all things for your ultimate good. That produces a joyful outlook that's based on how you look at life rather than on what is happening to you at that moment.

So don't just jump for joy. Live in it, and pray confidently for yourself and others—in spite of it all.

Heavenly Father, I want to joyously give thanks to You today for...

Sadness That Turns to Joy

Those who sow with tears will reap with songs of joy.
PSALM 126:5

A godly prayer life has many dynamics. Praising. Asking. Listening. Confessing. But when was the last time you truly grieved for your own missteps and waywardness or that of someone else?

In the Bible, the prophet Daniel grieved for his nation's stubborn nature. Even though they had been held captive by a neighboring superpower for seventy years, they would not turn to God. So Daniel pleaded with the Lord in prayer. He so identified with his nation's faults he confessed them as though he had committed them himself.

If your family or friends who are living in a way they shouldn't or are experiencing the consequences of their own stubborn ways, grieve for them in prayer. Take their needs before God in caring passion. If there's something you know is not right in your own life, pray for yourself with the same attitude. As surely as your tears bring sorrow, you can be confident that your mourning will turn to joy as God speaks and brings His restoration.

Dear Father, three people and circumstances that I can grieve in prayer for are...

God's Love Cubed

The Lord appeared to us in the past, saying:
"I have loved you with an everlasting love;
I have drawn you with unfailing kindness."
JEREMIAH 31:3

In the blissful days before video games, the Rubik's Cube was a puzzler's sensation. Remember it? Players would turn and twist the device until their wrists hurt in an attempt to have the rainbow of colors match perfectly on all six sides. Some figured out the cube rather quickly; others never could master it.

Many people believe God's vast love is just as complicated, but it isn't once you see it in the right dimension. A. T. Pierson, one of the greatest writers of the late nineteenth century, once observed that the Bible treats the love of God as a cube—having breadth and length, depth and height, a perfection of form. Every side of a cube is a perfect square, and from every angle it represents the same appearance.

God's love for you is flawless. Let that incredible realization encourage you in light of the challenges you're facing right now. The answers you seek in prayer to life's difficult puzzles will become clear as you focus on His perfect love.

God, thank You for showing Your love for me when...

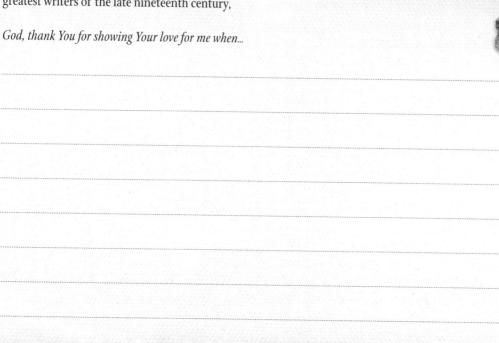

Delicious and Nutritious

Wisdom is like honey for you; if you find it, there is a future hope for you.
PROVERBS 24:14

You know the feeling. As the rich morsel leaves the fork and hits your tongue, the flavors of the decadent dessert transport you, if just for a moment, to a place of utter bliss. Whether fruity or chocolate, warm or cold, tasty treats like these are worth every bite. It's as though the calories don't even exist.

The Bible says that just as honey is sweet to your taste, so wisdom is delicious to your soul. But unlike that delightful dessert, wisdom is not only enjoyable—it also nourishes you. Two of the best ways to consume wisdom is through pleasant times of prayer and study of the Bible, God's letter to mankind. Plus, when you ask for and receive wisdom, God promises a future hope for you, one that will never be taken away. You become more confident as His wisdom feeds your spirit and dictates your outlook.

Today, seek your daily recommended allowance of godly wisdom. Let it bring joy and insight as you pray for yourself and others.

God, I need Your wisdom right now to help me to...

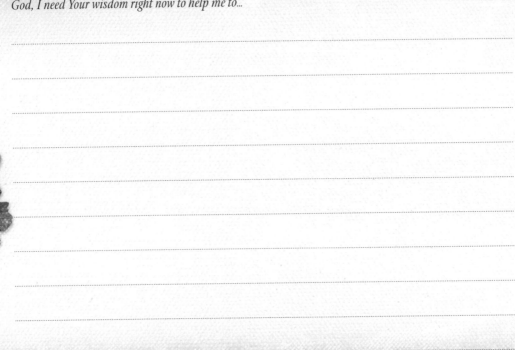

Ever-Present, Ever-Powerful

For the Kingdom of God is not just a lot of talk; it is living by God's power.
1 CORINTHIANS 4:20 NLT

When the trials and anxieties of the day surround you, how can you still be encouraged? The Bible says the love of God is poured into your heart in the person of the Holy Spirit. He reminds you of the hope that lies before you.

Think of it! Through prayer, you have personal access to the Creator of the universe on a daily, hourly, minute-by-minute basis. Because of that, you can take everything from your greatest worries to your smallest concerns to Him, knowing that He will listen and respond.

This gives you peace with God and, as a result, peace in and through all your life experiences. You know that He has always been ever-present and remains ever-powerful to address your every question.

God will not disappoint you! He loves you and took care of your past. He gives you security by caring for the present. His presence gives you hope for your future. Be encouraged and thank Him as you bring your needs before Him today in prayer.

I trust my future into Your hands, God, by trusting You with...

AUGUST 18

See as God Sees

Be imitators of God, as beloved children, and live in love, as Christ loved us and gave himself up for us.
EPHESIANS 5:1–2 NRSV

Each of us knows someone who appears to be unlovable. It may be a family member or a coworker; an old friend who recently looked us up online; or perhaps even a church authority or political leader. Can you picture this person for a moment?

Now that he or she is in the forefront of your mind, try to see that person in the same way God sees you: through eyes of love and concern, with an attitude of forgiveness and grace. That certainly changes things, doesn't it?

Remember, the same God who has the power to raise Jesus from the dead hears and honors your prayers, especially when they are spoken on behalf of someone who you do not love. Nothing is impossible for Him! Imagine picturing that unlovable person every morning and praying for him or her with God's heart. Ask for God's mercy on his or her life. Then ask God to change your heart so that you might see that individual more often through His eyes.

God, one unlovable person I'd like to pray for is...

His Job, Your Job

Oh, that my steps might be steady, keeping to the course you set.
PSALM 119:5 MSG

Right now, you may feel that the demands of your day are commandeering your life like a drill sergeant with a new recruit. As you look at that to-do list, you may also wonder if you're fulfilling any higher purpose for your life.

When you're trying to make sense of your myriad daily activities, you can find comfort in the Bible's promise that it is God's responsibility, not yours, to direct your steps. That's His job—and He'll do it lovingly, not harshly. Your job is to simply put Him first, knowing that as you do so, He's pledged to provide all your earthly needs.

Pray and ask for God's help for your day. Then, as you make and carry out your to-do list, He will guide you and fulfill His purpose in you. This puts you at ease as you go about your tasks. And, while seeking Him for yourself, pray also for your family, that God will accomplish His higher purposes in and through them.

I ask You, God, to help me accomplish...

Astonishing Sense of God

*In the fear of the LORD
there is strong confidence.*
PROVERBS 14:26 NKJV

Have you ever been to Niagara Falls or the Grand Canyon? Whether you're near the edge of the falls, enveloped by the thunder and spray of six million cubic feet of cascading water or standing at the rim of the canyon overcome with dizzying awe as you peer into the vast expanse of the seemingly bottomless gorge, both are akin to the "fear of the Lord." It isn't an unhealthy state of fright, but rather an overwhelming sense of God Himself.

But the fear of the Lord is more to you than an emotional response. It's also a state of being. It's something you *do*. The book of Ecclesiastes concludes by saying the "whole duty of man" can be summed up in this way: Fear God and keep His commandments.

The development of wisdom in your life starts with a loving reverence for God, characterized by submission to His Lordship and the guidance He gives you. Seek God's direction in prayer. What He says may astonish you.

God, I experience the "fear of the Lord" when...

Take Away the Mystery

The prayer of the upright is [God's] delight.
PROVERBS 15:8 KJV

Have you ever wondered if it makes a difference how many people pray for a situation? Does it matter whether you pray from a chair or on your knees, or in a church or on a mountain top? How often and how long should you pray?

The Bible teaches solitary prayer as well as public prayer, and it espouses prayer in all positions and all places. Jesus prayed privately and in groups. Israel gathered as a nation to pray. The Old Testament prophet Daniel prayed three times a day. God's people prayed standing up, kneeling, and on their faces.

Whatever mechanics you use, you can be assured that God's Spirit will help you pray in faith and according to His purposes. The model prayer given in the Bible includes thanksgiving, confession, and making requests. Whenever, wherever, and in whatever way is necessary, you can pray for your needs and for the needs of others in your life. So stop wondering. Prayer is as simple as talking to God and listening for His direction.

God, I seek Your nearness today as I pray for...

AUGUST 22

Lifeline of Rescue

Let us then approach God's throne of grace
with confidence, so that we may receive mercy
and find grace to help us in our time of need.
HEBREWS 4:16

"GAS PRICES SOAR." "US LAUNCHES MISSILE STRIKE." "THOUSANDS KILLED IN TSUNAMI." Headlines and news shows include reports on war, floods, abuses, and scandal. If you're like many, you listen and ache inside.

When all this bad news merges with your personal dilemmas—financial stress, family issues, job problems—you may become overwhelmed and do almost anything to medicate the pain. You may work more, shop more, eat more, or drink more. Yet underneath the obsessive behavior, you long for rescue, for someone to understand and help.

God is that someone. He cares that you are surrounded by bad news. He's given you prayer as a lifeline. The Bible says you can approach God with confidence, knowing you will receive mercy and find grace to help in your time of need. Today, the world around you, and even your personal life, may be going through tough, trying times. Tell God in prayer that you believe in Him and accept His help when your heart feels heavy.

God, the concerns I turn over to You today are...

Pull an All-Nighter

My eyes stay open through the watches of the night, that I may meditate on your promises.
PSALM 119:148

Have you ever had a decision to make and, after weeks of contemplation, you still had no idea what to do? You may have made lists of all the pros and cons. Or perhaps you did research or asked for advice. You may have even whispered (or screamed) a prayer or two.

When it was time for Jesus to choose His disciples, did He make a list of pros and cons? Matthew is faithful but unpopular. Peter is passionate but impulsive. James and John are devoted, but they have a mom who is politically ambitious and a dad with a quick temper.

The Bible says that before He selected His disciples, Jesus spent the night praying. Sometimes you need answers beyond your knowledge and understanding. That's when you need to spend time with God; not only speaking, but taking the time to listen.

Pray determinedly, all night if you have to, for the important decisions you need to make, then listen carefully for God's direction and obey wholeheartedly.

This week I'm asking You, God, to guide my decisions about...

....

....

....

....

....

....

....

Truthful Lips

Lying lips are abomination to the LORD: but they that deal truly are his delight.
PROVERBS 12:22 KJV

Within the pages of the Bible, God has given us one condition for hearing our prayers. We must come before Him wrapped in a robe of truth. We can't hustle God. We cannot persuade Him with fast talk, persuasive words, or empty promises.

God responds to one thing—a truthful heart. That's a heart that quickly owns up to mistakes, a heart that throws aside disguises, a heart that is free of deceit and ulterior motives. Because you are God's child, He expects your heart to be like His, and His never wavers from the path of truth and honesty.

When you pray, come before the heavenly Father with an honest heart, nothing held back or concealed. What you have to tell Him might not be pretty but it will be real. And that's all He really wants from you. As you open yourself up to God, He will open Himself up to you. You will feel His presence and a wonderful sense of comfort and well-being.

God, these are the things I want to be honest with You about...

....

....

....

....

....

....

....

Wise and Intimate Friend

Wisdom is a tree of life to those who embrace her;
happy are those who hold her tightly.
PROVERBS 3:18 NLT

When growing up, gossip, scheming, and the silent treatment between siblings is commonplace. Sibling rivalry can rise to great heights—or depths, depending on your perspective. Moments of genuine love and forgiveness come sporadically at best.

But as they mature into adulthood, the bond between siblings can become a unique and extremely loyal union, an intimate friendship only they truly understand and appreciate. In the Bible, we are told to seek the same kind of close kinship with wisdom. But how do you do that?

To have fellowship with *wisdom*, you must spend every moment you can nurturing your relationship with God, your ultimate and fully reliable source of wisdom.

Over the next month, determine to spend at least one additional hour per week with God. It could be by Bible reading, prayer, worship, or any combination of these. Enrich your time with Him, deepen your bond. As you do, *wisdom* will be your intimate companion—unique, loyal, and inseparable.

God, I want to spend extra time with You this week to...

Partnering for the Impossible

Give and it will be given to you: good measure,
pressed down, shaken together, and running over.
LUKE 6:38 NKJV

Have you ever voiced any of these reasons for not reaching out to others? "I'm not gifted [or educated]." "I'm too young [or too busy]." "I'll wait until I make a bigger salary." Or, "I've had my turn. Let the new generation do it." Perhaps you feel you have valid explanations for saying no to specific opportunities to serve.

In the Bible, when Jesus' disciples suggested that He send the crowd home, Jesus said, "They don't need to go. Just give them some food."

Jesus' team didn't have the means to feed ten thousand people. Yet Jesus seems to say, "Give Me what you have. I'll increase it and give it back to you so you can share it with others."

Instead of focusing on what you don't have, make a list of what you do have. Then ask God to create opportunities for you to put that list into action. Let your prayers reveal opportunities to serve. Move beyond your reluctance and partner with God for what seems impossible.

God, the characteristics I can offer You for service to others are...

God's Biggest Fan

O God, you are my God, I seek you, my soul thirsts for you;
my flesh faints for you, as in a dry and weary land where there is no water.
PSALM 63:1 NRSV

The sports fan is an interesting animal. He or she may not recall vital information such as his ATM number or the location of his car keys, but his brain will instantly conjure up Magic Johnson's alma mater, the co-MVPs of Super Bowl XII, or the team the Dodgers beat the last time they won the World Series. Why does this phenomenon occur? Because people tend to easily remember those things that bring them joy and relaxation.

Knowing God and communicating with Him in prayer should be, at minimum, as pleasurable to you as, say, an evening of watching game highlights is to the sports fan. Actually, recalling what God reveals to you in your prayer time and applying it to who you are is to be your delight!

Don't let your relationship with God and praying to Him be mere duty. Allow God's wisdom to be your life's fun and joy—and join His fan club!

God, I enjoy being with You because...

From Frustration to Faith

Let us draw near to God with a sincere heart and with the full assurance that faith brings.
HEBREWS 10:22

"Just have a little faith." You know the person giving you this advice means well. Still, it's not easy to do when things seem so messed up.

The Bible says that faith is confidence in God's ability to complete what He started. It is trusting that God's in charge; that He will do what you can't. Though you try with all the discernment you can muster, you'll never know exactly what tomorrow holds. You probably wish you could. It's especially frustrating when well-intentioned attempts through your prayers to direct your family, church, the economy, or the government fail to produce the results you want.

Yet frustration can give way to faith. Pray that God will help you loosen your grip on people, things, and circumstances and trust Him more for what you cannot do. Pray also that your family members, friends, coworkers, and even national leaders will release their frustrations to God, who is able to see them through any difficulty with just a little faith.

God, some of the issues I need to loosen my grip on are...

Replacing Misplaced Trust

The fear of man brings a snare, but whoever trusts in the LORD shall be safe.
PROVERBS 29:25 NKJV

Sometimes people become obsessed with performance, work, and success because they feel driven to please another human being. When this person is happy, life is enjoyable. But if this individual becomes displeased, life takes a nosedive.

This is a painful way to live. In fact, this people-pleasing philosophy can begin to feel cursed or parched, leading to depression or burnout when dreams concerning this person fail to come true. God says that joy and peace come when you shift your ultimate trust from people to Him. You can learn to care, give, and love others out of the freedom and joy of God's acceptance.

Today, release any misplaced trust you may have and tell God in prayer that you've decided to put your complete confidence in His love and purpose for you. While you pray that you'll not be unduly swayed by others' opinion and approval, also pray that your friends and coworkers will also find the benefit of trusting God first.

I reaffirm my trust in You today, God, by...

Waiting for the Evidence

The Lord is good; his steadfast love endures for ever, and his faithfulness to all generations.
PSALM 100:5 NRSV

Do you ever find it hard to understand the things that happen to you after you decide to put your faith in Him? You want to believe that He is working in your circumstances, but you see little clear-cut evidence.

You're not alone. Over the course of time, many people have faced situations that seemed impossible to overcome. From the ancient days of Noah's flood to the modern days of worldwide terrorism, people have faced threats that birthed fear and hopelessness. Yet history is also replete with examples of God performing the miraculous for those who love Him.

You can be assured that God will keep His promises to you. Ask Him in prayer to give you the courage to remain faithful against overwhelming odds. Believe that He is helping you, even when you don't understand or when change doesn't happen as rapidly as you wish. Trust that He is in control of what is happening. Pray also for your family members who need to see that God is their assurance in difficulty.

I will believe You, God, for seemingly impossible needs such as...

....

....

....

....

....

....

....

Heavenly Project Managers

My beloved, be steadfast, immovable, always excelling in the work of the Lord, because you know that in the Lord your labor is not in vain.

1 CORINTHIANS 15:58 NRSV

Imagine a huge project you may have worked on with a friend; perhaps putting on a party, planning a wedding, or going on a road trip together. If you worked together well, you may have created a lasting friendship.

As you pray for yourself and for others, think of it as a project you and God are working on together. The Bible tells you three ways you can get along with God as you work with Him. You're to be joyful while you trust in Him to do the brunt of the work and to produce quality results. You're to endure with a good attitude through the tough times. And you're to be faithful, dependable, and committed in prayer until your prayer project is complete.

As you work with God on this enormous project, developing these qualities as you go, you have a unique opportunity to create a deep, intimate, lasting bond with Him.

God, some prayer projects I'd like to undertake with You are...

A Symphony of Prayer

Where two or three gather in my name, there am I with them.
MATTHEW 18:20

You know it when you hear it. A piece of music, perfectly orchestrated, sends you on a wonderful aural journey in which you actually feel the impact of the conductor's baton and sense what the composer might have experienced as she created her art.

Something similar awaits you as you pray. When the Bible mentions people being "joined together" in prayer, it is a compound of two words meaning to "rush along" and "in unison." The image is musical; a number of notes which, while different, harmonize in pitch and tone. Like instruments under the direction of a master Conductor, so God blends together two or more people to accomplish the mighty work of prayer.

So it was in biblical times, and so it is today. Commit to pray in unity with others for whatever needs and concerns you have for yourself, your friends, or even your neighborhood. You'll make spiritual music that'll please the Lord and change the lives of those impacted by your sweet intercessions.

God, I will pray together this week with...

The God Who Remembers

I will remember the deeds of the LORD;
yes, I will remember your miracles of long ago.
PSALM 77:11

You almost certainly have one or more photo albums, scrapbooks, or treasure boxes in your home, and you likely count them among your most prized possessions. They are all creative ways to share memories and store dreams. Photo albums recall events past. Scrapbooks reminisce of experiences gone by. Treasure boxes remind you of wishes and hopes for tomorrow.

In the Bible, there are a number of instances when people called God to remembrance. They were not implying that God had forgotten. Instead, they were setting the stage to make a request in the present based on a promise in the past.

God certainly knows your past experiences and what your future will be. He also appreciates your dreams and aspirations. But most important, God keeps you in His mind, remaining aware and vigilant of your needs today.

Remember that as you bring your concerns to Him in prayer. Recall His promises and how He has kept them in the past. Then pray with renewed confidence.

God, remember Your promises to me today as I pray for...

September 3

A Turn in Perspective

Our light and momentary troubles are achieving for us an eternal glory that far outweighs them all.
2 Corinthians 4:17

A scene in the classic movie *Steel Magnolias* shows four women gathered around their dear friend at the gravesite of her daughter. The mother is distraught and cannot quit shouting, "Why? Why did my daughter have to die?" Then one of the older women cracks a joke. Her friends look at her stunned, but after a short pause, they all burst out laughing.

What changed their outlook? Their thoughts were given a different focus! In the Bible, we read that King David often felt utterly forsaken,

sorrowful, and under attack. He'd even question God, "How long will it be this way?" Yet David's thoughts always turned toward the benefits of God in his life, especially the undeserved and unfailing mercy God gave to him.

When you have trying times, change your thinking. No matter how bleak circumstances appear, pray that you may have God's perspective, seeing life as He does. Reflect the joy in your heart for God's bountiful blessings. Praise Him. Then pray with thanksgiving.

I thank You, God, and pray for new perspective concerning...

_____

_____

_____

_____

_____

_____

_____

Rest Stop Required

I will refresh the weary and satisfy the faint.
JEREMIAH 31:25

When you're exhausted, you have less control over your emotions. Depression descends more easily. Worry grips you more doggedly. Temptations can catch you unawares. Do these scenarios sound familiar to you?

Sleeplessness and exhaustion have happened to many people, including one of the Bible's greatest prophets, Elijah. He had combated paganism for three years, went head-to-head against a cabal of false prophets, and God had given him victory. But he was at the end of his rope. Tired and fearful of threats against his life, Elijah fled—and God made him rest. It was only after that time of regeneration that God spoke to Elijah and helped him move forward with his life.

If you're waiting for specific direction from God but don't seem to be getting anywhere, ask Him to help you let go of all your burdens so you can rest *first*. Once you are refreshed, you will be better able to listen for His still, small voice, and obey His direction.

God, please help me to find rest tonight as I give You...

SEPTEMBER 5

How's Your Hospitality?

*Do not neglect to show
hospitality to strangers.*
HEBREWS 13:2 NRSV

How do you react when strangers knock on your door? In this day and age, you would likely wonder what they're selling or why they're bothering you. You certainly wouldn't let them inside, right?

In ancient times, things were different. Reputation was largely determined by hospitality. If you were appropriately neighborly, you'd greet guests before they even reached your door, provide food and drink, and let them know it was an honor to serve them. You'd treat them as you would treat your own loved ones and care for them as sacrificially as possible.

Of course, we live in a very different world, one where safety issues must be considered. Still, look around and you will find many opportunities to be hospitable. You can reach out to the needy, the homeless, and new arrivals in your neighborhood, to name just a few. Pray that you would be welcoming and sensitive to their needs. Then serve to the best of your ability. Most of all, bless them with your prayers that God will meet the needs you do not see.

Lord God, change my heart and make me more...

Astronomic, Titanic God

God's love is meteoric, his loyalty astronomic,
his purpose titanic, his verdicts oceanic.
Yet in his largeness nothing gets lost.
PSALM 36:5 MSG

Who are you? What are you doing? Simple questions, right—yet sometimes you don't always have the answers as life stretches and challenges you.

But God knows who He is and what He is doing. Even better, He knows exactly what you need for your life today. God decides what's best, and His answers are always right. And the best part is He is a personal, intimate God. There is nothing too big, too difficult, or too painful for Him to handle. Human beings are limited in what they can do, but not God. His love and His power have no boundaries and no barriers. He is always there to help as much as you will allow Him to.

God is real, and He is always lovingly watching over you. As you pray for the needs of those you love today, ask Him to enable them to trust His purposes for their lives. Then ask God to accomplish His purposes in you and provide the answers you need.

God, the simple but big questions I have about my life are...

Apple of His Eye

Keep me as the apple of your eye; hide me in the shadow of your wings.
PSALM 17:8

What do we do for protection when a severe storm comes? We head for the basement or board up our house and seek shelter elsewhere. When fired upon, our military men and women seek cover behind a building or in a cave or call for air cover from other forces.

What did people in the Bible do when they were in danger and under attack? The Israelite king David often acknowledged that God's words kept him on the right path. He also expressed his confidence that God would answer his prayers and guard him by His strong right hand. David even boldly asked to be kept as the apple of God's eye, a common Hebrew metaphor for protection against oppression. He knew that as a bird hides its young under its wings, God would provide refuge for him.

He'll do the same for you as you keep your eyes upon Him. Pray for God's protective shield for yourself and those in your life who are in harm's way.

I ask for Your protection, God, for the following people...

Are You Hungry?

*Blessed are those who hunger and thirst
for righteousness, for they will be filled.*
MATTHEW 5:6 NRSV

How do you feel when you're hungry? Is it a gnawing? Churning? Or just a sense in your gut that you need to eat?

Most people are good at ignoring the signs of hunger. Sadly, some do so because their circumstances demand it. Hunger pangs are a gift from God that drive us to replenish our bodies with the nutrients they need. This is His loving protection and care, meant to keep us strong and healthy.

You can also experience spiritual hunger pangs—the longing for God that can only be satisfied by feasting on the Bible, His love letter to mankind—and by spending satisfying moments in prayer. When you gratify your spiritual appetite with anything besides God, you risk addiction, spiritual disease, or worse. Only God satisfies this craving!

As you seek God in prayer today, ask Him to send a churning, stirring hunger for God into the hearts of those you love.

I ask You, God, to increase my hunger for Your direction concerning...

Resting by the Rock

Let us not be weary in well doing: for in due
season we shall reap, if we faint not.
GALATIANS 6:9 KJV

Have you seen salmon swimming upstream? These amazingly driven fish are known to rest from the pummeling effects of the current by hiding behind a rock. As the water surges around the stone, the fish stays in the calm spot created by the bulk of the rock. Once refreshed, it moves back into the flow, revived for the next challenge, whether prey, fisherman, or grizzly bear.

If you sometimes feel weary in your "well doing" as you pray, perhaps it's time to draw near to God, the Rock, and allow the current to flow past while you rest. You honor God when you care for your spiritual life by taking refuge in Him. You don't need to do anything during these times except just be with Him.

Your dedication to prayer for yourself and others is hard work. As you head into the rest of this week, take time to rest in Him. You'll then be renewed as you continue to pray faithfully.

God, I ask You to refresh me especially in these concerns...

Assurance for the Future

*Don't get worked up about what may
or may not happen tomorrow.*
MATTHEW 6:34 MSG

It's natural to fear the future. We wonder how our lives might change and what we might lose. God has never promised that the future will be simple. In fact, the Bible, in its final book, paints a grim picture of the last days of our planet.

What God *does* promise is that those who place their trust in Him have nothing to fear. Like a loving father, He will be there to encourage, protect, defend, and bless. And you can be certain that nothing will catch God off guard, nothing will take Him by surprise. He knows the beginning from the end, and He will see you through every day, every hour, every minute.

When you feel yourself being drawn into fear for what will happen in the future, present yourself to God and ask Him to brush your fear away and fill your heart with confidence in His loving care. He will never fail you. You can be absolutely certain of that even in the face of an uncertain future.

God, I will put my faith in You for...

Protection from Unseen Terror

In peace I will lie down and sleep, for you alone, LORD, make me dwell in safety.
PSALM 4:8

Do you remember your simplest fears as a child? Did you shudder every time a spider crept across the ceiling? Or did mighty claps of thunder send you scurrying to your parents' bed?

On September 11, 2001, Americans experienced terrible fright when terrorists flew planes into huge buildings and thousands died. In such extraordinary circumstances, you come to the end of your own resources and find yourself utterly reliant on God and others. In the face of such difficulty, you turn to Him with the same helplessness as a child in a raging storm.

God promises His very presence in fright or joy alike. You do not know when or if terrorists will strike again, but you do know that your prayers serve as a great shield, protecting you from unseen terror and guarding your heart. You can pray for those you love, even your nation, with confidence and peace in those moments when you fear. God promises to hear and answer those prayers as you trust fully in Him.

Heavenly Father, protect me from my fears, especially...

Seen Safely Home

*Forgetting what is behind and straining toward what is ahead, I press on toward the
goal to win the prize for which God has called me heavenward in Christ Jesus.*
PHILIPPIANS 3:13–14

Ever felt like your life has taken a wrong turn?
We all have. When that happens, the Bible
encourages us to forget what's behind and press
on toward the goal ahead. In other words, once
we get off track, we should find out how to reach
our destination from our present location, not
from our original starting point.

Too often in life, we waste time stewing over
wrong turns instead of finding Plan B. We need
to get out the "map"—which is the Bible—and
reorient ourselves. We may end up taking a
different route, maybe not as effeciently as the
first, but we'll get there just the same.

No matter how many wrong turns you've
taken, determine to pursue God and His wisdom
from your current position. Don't fret about how
you got there. Just determine to get back on track
through your faithful and unswerving prayers,
trusting God to see you safely home.

God, guide my path today as I make decisions about...

In the Flow

I instruct you in the way of wisdom and lead you along straight paths.
PROVERBS 4:11

Perhaps you have one adorning your home or office, trickling with relaxing ease. Those soothing water fountains come in all shapes and sizes and are marketed under the guise of stress relief. If you have one, you know they can work wonders. Not only are they calming to the ear, they're also enjoyable to watch: the tiny stream perpetually flowing where it's directed, never wavering.

Keep that image fresh in your mind as you consider your life being guided and directed by God as a result of your prayers. Sometimes His leading is straight and unimpeded, like being peacefully poured down a set of perfectly placed stones. Other times the events in our lives bend this way and that, His purposes worming us back and forth on a dizzying path. Yet either way, we can be certain that God, by His insight, will steer us in the way of wisdom and place us in the direction He wishes us to go.

Allow God to speak to your heart and then stay in the life-giving flow of His wisdom as you pray.

Let me confidently and peacefully pray, God, for...

Open House for God

Do you not know that your body is a temple
of the Holy Spirit within you, which you have
from God, and that you are not your own?
1 CORINTHIANS 6:19 NRSV

Imagine a family moves into your neighborhood. Their house is brand new, but over time it begins to show the effects of their careless lifestyle. The yard is littered with trash, the front porch in shambles.

Then another family buys the house and moves in. They immediately paint, clean the yard, and repair the porch. You can hardly believe it's the same house. What happened? There is a significant improvement in the appearance because different people now live there.

There will also be a dramatic change in your life once you start trusting God because there will be a perfect new resident living inside you: His Spirit. Is your spiritual house in disrepair? Does it need restoration? If so, make your heart an "Open House" for God's inspection. Let His Spirit renew your hope in Him. Then reflect that change in your prayers for God's love and kindness to be renewed in the lives of those around you.

God, renew me today by changing my attitude about...

Seeing the Future

The LORD is trustworthy in all he promises and faithful in all he does.
PSALM 145:13

Four thousand years ago, God asked His faithful follower Abraham to leave his home country and live as an immigrant in another land. He went from living in a house to living in a tent, where he remained for the remainder of his life. He ranched as a free-range grazer, being shuffled around at the whim of his landholding neighbors, ending up with the less desirable fields, and scrambling to find enough water. When his wife died, he had to buy a burial plot at twenty times the going price.

But God told him to walk the length and breadth of the land. "All of this," God said, "I will give to you." Abraham died, owning no land but his own tomb. Yet he was able to see beyond his natural life to the great work God would someday accomplish: the entire land God had promised was, indeed, given to his descendants.

If you're praying for something and you don't see any results, don't give up. God always keeps His promises.

God, grant me persistent faith concerning...

Waiting for His Very Best

Be brave and courageous. Yes, wait patiently for the LORD.
PSALM 27:14 NLT

God tends to answer every prayer in one of three ways: yes, no, and not yet. When He says yes, we are jubilant. When He says no, we may be disappointed, but accepting in time. But when the Lord says not yet, it tends to throw us off because it means we have to wait for His answer—and no one likes to wait.

Perhaps you've experienced one of those waiting times in your life. They can be frustrating beyond words, and sometimes you might even be tempted to give up and claim a no rather than continue to wait. At other times, you might try to hurry your answer by overriding God's timing with your own. That always spells disaster.

Waiting will probably never be your first choice, but you can choose how you wait. Pray for strength and courage and perseverance to wait for God's perfect timing and His best for your life. God's intention is not to torture you but to bring all the aspects of your life together in perfect harmony. Trust Him to do just that.

I will be patient, God, as I wait for Your answer to...

Break Down the Wall

God...reconciled us to himself through Christ and gave us the ministry of reconciliation.
2 CORINTHIANS 5:18

Have you ever been so mad at someone that you didn't want to apologize for your actions or words? Did you ever need to ask your child for forgiveness for your angry outburst, but hesitated? There is a wall between the two of you, a barrier that, left unaddressed, could eventually destroy that relationship.

This is where God's incredible love for you makes an impact. He took the initiative to provide, at terrible cost, the ultimate avenue for restoration. He sent His Son. Belief that Jesus loves you, forgives you, and lives in you restores you to a harmonious relationship with God and enables you to then practice that same restoration in your life's most important relationships. Forgiveness is possible because you have been forgiven.

What could give you greater joy than to break down that wall? Strive to live Jesus' love in all that you do toward others. Apologize when you need to and seek restoration—starting with your prayers. Discover the pleasure of being at peace with others and with God.

Help me to apologize, God, to...

Finding the Missing Piece

*If you look for it as for silver and search for it as
for hidden treasure, then you will understand the fear
of the Lord and find the knowledge of God.*

PROVERBS 2:4–5

Have you ever worked a jigsaw puzzle and found yourself searching desperately for that one last piece to complete a section of the picture? You repeatedly scan the table, but you just can't find it, even though you know it's right there in front of you. When you finally discover the elusive missing piece, you want to sound a trumpet! You finally put the section together. You've completed part of a beautiful picture by filling that empty space with the one and only piece of the puzzle that was designed to fill it.

In the larger picture of life, many people look everywhere for something to fill that God-shaped space He created within them. Yet nothing they try to put in that space ever quite fits, leaving their life picture incomplete. Yet your prayers can help them find that missing piece and discover the love of God as you have.

Today, let God infuse your intercessions for others. You never know how powerfully He may use you.

God, give me a tender heart toward others as I pray for...

SEPTEMBER 19

Be Desperately Dedicated

To those who by persistence
in doing good seek glory, honor,
and immortality, he will give eternal life.
ROMANS 2:7

Is God asleep when it comes to answering your prayers? Are you having a hard time being devoted to prayer? If you're not careful, discouragement can slip in like a fog and chill your prayer life.

In the Bible, Jesus told a story to keep you from losing heart when you pray. It's about a woman who was so determined to have her voice heard by the local judge that she did not allow herself to give up or become disheartened. The woman was desperate to have the judge rule in her favor, and he finally did because of her persistence.

Today you may be in need of the help only God can provide, and He is the only source that can make you what you ought to be. He's also the only one who can change the hearts of those for whom you pray. You may not witness the outcome of your consistent prayer—at times God works outside of your view—but He wants you to be desperately dedicated as you seek Him. Let Him find you faithful!

I want to be more persistent, God, as I pray for...

Your Foremost Desire

People who are ruled by their desires think only of themselves.
Everyone who is ruled by the Holy Spirit thinks about spiritual things.
ROMANS 8:5 CEV

Have you ever been around a child with a king-sized case of the "gimmies"? Whether you were the child's parent or just an unfortunate bystander, you probably remember how quickly he or she became a giant irritant to everyone within earshot. The only saving grace was that everyone knew the perpetrator was just a kid. Eventually most children grow out of their immature behavior.

Do you find yourself acting this way at times? It's easy to do, especially when there's an unfulfilled longing in your heart. Sometimes a simple change in focus can make all the difference. When you, in prayer, adjust your desires to become those that God wants for you, your "gimmies" go from selfish to self*less*, and you find yourself more content in what you have and who you are.

As you talk to God, constantly guard yourself against greed, emotional or material. Give your "gimmies" to Him, desire God above all else—and enjoy the blessing of knowing you are growing in maturity.

God, I ask you to help me no longer covet...

Listen to the Teacher

I will instruct you and teach you in the way you should go;
I will counsel you with my loving eye on you.
PSALM 32:8

Think back to your favorite teacher in school. Because of that person's character and loving qualities, it was the one class you hated to miss. You might have hated the subject, even disliked most of your fellow students, but it didn't matter. The teacher connected with you so strongly, motivated you so completely, that you couldn't wait to dive in to the next assignment.

As an adult, you may no longer have access to such a teacher, but you can communicate daily with someone even wiser. God longs to be with you in a unique and personal way. His loving qualities continue to draw you in and, like any good teacher, He is excited when you are attentive and interested in what He has to say.

As you pray today, don't just speak, but be careful to listen to what God is teaching you. Allow Him to thoroughly influence and direct your thoughts and attitudes, and your faith will grow.

God, the steps I will take to tune out the distractions in my life are...

Lower Your Stress Points

I will greatly rejoice in the LORD, my soul shall be joyful in my God.
ISAIAH 61:10 NKJV

Imagine taking a stress test ascribing points to each of your situations and discovering your score was in the danger zone. Ever feel that way as life presses in?

If today's psychiatrists had designated stress points to the problems the apostle Paul faced in the Bible (shipwrecks, imprisonment, starvation, physical exhaustion, etc.), his score would've been so far off the scale they would have expected him to disintegrate. But Paul said that, despite his troubles, he had boundless joy!

Happiness (based on circumstances) goes up and down like a thermometer. True joy comes through faith in God, knowing that He loves you, answers your prayers, and works things for your good.

If your life is filled with bad news, turn your mind to God's good news and thank Him for His benefit in your life. You'll probably find there are more benefits than you think. Then, once you have prayed for yourself, ask God to work in the lives of your loved ones, that they'll find true joy in His eternal truths.

God, I give thanks to You today for the wonderful benefits of...

What He Wants

*In the path of your judgments,
O Lord, we wait for you; your name and
your renown are the soul's desire.*
ISAIAH 26:8 NRSV

Have you ever promised a child they'd soon receive something wonderful? When children are filled with anticipation like that, they become quite relentless, asking for it over and over until it becomes a reality.

What are you waiting for with anticipation? Perhaps it's an answer to an immensely important prayer that's weighing heavily on your heart. As fast as time normally flies, it can surely seem to drag when you're waiting for something you desperately want. But keep in mind that God often brings unexpected divine appointments your way during those times of waiting that will positively change the course of countless lives, including your own.

God is also waiting. He's waiting for you to join Him in bringing more and more people into fellowship with Him, something you do each time you intercede for others and for the world you live in. Focus less on what you want and more on what He wants to do through you as you seek Him in prayer.

God, show me how You want to use my prayers today...

More Wonderful Reality

We have gifts that differ according to the grace given to us.
ROMANS 12:6 NRSV

Everyone is gifted with different talents. You may have a gift for speaking in public. Someone else may have a gift for writing letters of encouragement. God has also given every person a specific opportunity for service to others. And even if you think your gift is small or trivial, it could be the very thing that God employs to draw someone to His love.

Yet the delight of using that gift pales in comparison to the greater gift of eternal life. In the Bible, we read that Jesus sent out seventy-two of His followers to serve in the towns and villages He was about to visit. They were thrilled by the success they were having, but Jesus quickly put things in perspective, saying that their joy should not rest in the supernatural, but in the more wonderful reality of their salvation.

Today, appreciate your talents and abilities, but don't find your happiness in them. Thank God that you have been forgiven. Then pray that He would use you—and your talents and abilities—to help others discover His forgiving love.

Allow me today, God, to show Your love to...

Finding Heavenly Brainpower

Who may ascend the mountain of the LORD?
...The one who...does not trust
in an idol or swear by a false god.
PSALM 24:3–4

Sure, he could sing and dance, but the Scarecrow in MGM's *The Wizard of Oz* lacked one indispensable item—a brain. Without that, he didn't feel capable to deduce the sum of the square root of an isosceles triangle, or anything else for that matter.

Sometimes we mistakenly put our hopes into things that make no sense, some kind of idol. Not only can they not speak, but idols can't see, hear, smell, feel, or walk. They're utterly brainless. Not mincing words, the Bible twice calls idols "worthless," and the book of Psalms goes further, saying that those who have idols "will be like them."

What are you relying upon today? A TV program; a political agenda; your financial portfolio; that next promotion? Don't listen to anything other than God for direction. Only God has the insight you need for your life's walk. Turn your ear to God by conversing with Him in prayer and enjoy the brainpower of His indispensible wisdom.

God, help me to identify anything I've set up as an idol and remove it by...

Rising Above It All

He will yet fill your mouth with laughter and your lips with shouts of joy.
JOB 8:21

Happiness is like a slippery eel. Just when you think you have hold of it, it slides from your grasp and slithers away. When the situation changes, there goes your happiness!

Joy is different. The world can be crashing down around you, yet you can be joyful when you place your trust in God. It's possible that you have allowed circumstances to rob you of the joy God wants you to have. It's easy to lose joy if you look only at what's happening around you. The Bible says we are to be joyful always. God wants you to live above your circumstances rather than under them by keeping your eyes on Him.

Right now, thank the Lord for allowing the current conditions and events in your life, realizing He has something for you to learn or accomplish through them. Then pray with that same attitude for the circumstances your friends and family are facing, knowing God is still accomplishing His purposes for them as well. Have a joyful heart in Him, and don't let it slip away.

God, please help me in circumstances that are troubling me today such as...

Individually Perfect and Pleasing

Be transformed by the renewing of your minds, so that you may discern what is the will of God.
ROMANS 12:2 NRSV

"What is God's purpose for my life?" How many times have you asked this question of yourself? You come to a crossroads, and you pray for wisdom about which direction to take, but the answer eludes you. Finally, you choose what you believe is the right course, only to discover disastrous consequences at the end of the road.

The invaluable lessons of life are often found on paths less traveled. Whatever road you take, know that God will direct your steps every inch of the way. His purpose is good for you *individu-ally* and no one else. It is perfect for you. And whatever His specific purpose is for your life, you can believe it is pleasing to Him.

The Bible encourages you to be transformed by renewing your mind so that you will be able to "test and approve" what God's will is for you. You do this by seeking Him in prayer and asking Him to affect your thinking, to give you His thoughts and assurance that His will is good, perfect, and pleasing.

Heavenly Father, reveal Your purposes for me as I pray...

Your Continual Choice

Very early in the morning, while it was still dark, Jesus got up,
left the house and went off to a solitary place, where he prayed.
MARK 1:35

To live on earth is to walk the confines of space and time. You cannot enjoy the quaintness of peaceful Lake Tahoe and experience the fervor of California's wavier shores at the same time.

Each life choice is the same. Get married now or establish your career? Stay home with the kids or take that extra job? With unlimited time you could perhaps do it all. But your days are numbered. That's why priorities are so important.

Jesus had a little more than thirty years to walk this planet. How He lived reveals a lot about godly priorities. He visited the poor. He played with children. He invested all of Himself in others. And He regularly slipped off to be alone and pray. It was a continual choice.

The needs of the people were great, the crowds persistent—yet Jesus held communication with His Father as vital. Follow in His thoughtful footsteps and rediscover your solitary, daily place with Him.

God, I choose to spend more time with You by reprioritizing...

Godly Voice Recognition

My sheep listen to my voice; I know them, and they follow me.
JOHN 10:27

When a mother shopping in a crowded mall suddenly hears a small voice crying out for attention, she instantly knows whether or not it is her child because she automatically recognizes the voice. It doesn't matter if the child is lost or hungry, close or far away. She knows that voice and immediately responds, no matter where it's coming from.

Likewise, when you pray to God, He will recognize your voice, no matter where you are. There's one example from the Bible where the apostle Paul and his cohorts paused to pray on the beach. First century Christians, for the most part, met in homes or in borrowed rooms. They had no church buildings or cathedrals. They studied, worshiped, and prayed where they could, when they could.

Prayer is a conversation with God. It's not an event to be confined to any one location. Since God is in all places, know that He is with you and knows your voice—in a church, on the beach, or even driving down the highway.

God, hear my voice as I come before You with...

Praying with Fragility

Trust in him at all times, you people; pour out your hearts to him, for God is our refuge.
PSALM 62:8

If humans came with an instruction book, you'd see labels like FRAGILE or HANDLE WITH CARE stamped prominently on the cover. This is shown in the fascinating way the men and women in the Bible prayed. Their vulnerability is there for all to see. They lament and cry out, begging God to know them. Then, before it's all done, they're singing praises about His faithfulness.

The writer of most of the Psalms, David, knew God was listening to Him. In his heartfelt prayers, King David learned of God's dependability, discovered that he could rely on God's kindness, and waited with anticipation for God's answer, even if His response was going to be different than David wanted.

The Lord enjoys this process. Relationship and communication are His inventions, and He loves to live them out with us. Today, share your deepest feelings with God as you seek Him in prayer. No matter how fragile you're feeling, He'll prove the reliability of your trust in Him—and He'll handle you with the utmost care.

God, I will trust You today with my heartfelt prayers for...

Finding God in the Busyness

He will never leave you nor forsake you.
DEUTERONOMY 31:6

Life tends to carry us at warp speed. Whether it's playing chauffer to the kids—a part-time job in itself!—while working full time or juggling family and friend obligations, slowing down can seem nearly impossible. How do you fit prayer into your schedule?

Remember that God doesn't live in a box, waiting for you to pull Him out so you can spend some quality time together. In fact, you don't even need to make an appointment with Him. No matter where you are, no matter what you're doing, God is with you. Busy schedule and all.

Envision Him sitting shotgun with you in the car or in yet another meeting. Acknowledge His presence and enjoy Him. Imagine Him laughing with you when someone tells a joke. You can even hold a silent conversation with Him in the middle of a crowd. Then, when a brief lull finally appears, relax in His presence. Don't let your busy schedule prevent you from enjoying the God who promises to never leave you nor forsake you.

Dear God, I know You're in the middle of my busyness when...

Making Time for God

Seek the Lord while he may be found,
call upon him while he is near.
ISAIAH 55:6 NRSV

While God exists in the middle of our busy schedules, He still longs for more than a quiet acknowledgement or a brief whispered prayer. He longs for you.

Avoid beating yourself up when you push God to the margins of your life. All too often, feelings of guilt and condemnation prevent us from reestablishing contact with Him.

If your calendar tends to dictate how you spend your time, then schedule God into your calendar. You don't need to clear an hour or two, just make Him your early morning or late afternoon fifteen-minute appointment. If you can't spare fifteen minutes, even five minutes will do. Scheduling in advance will allow you to build your schedule around Him.

Then when you're together, avoid wasting time explaining why it took so long to meet—just enjoy Him. Bask in His presence. Share with Him your innermost feelings. Listen. Over time, you'll discover that your brief appointments with God will begin reordering your priorities and move Him from the margins of your life to the center.

Dear God, I would like to meet with You at...

OCTOBER 3

Turning Down the Volume

After the earthquake came a fire, but the LORD was not in the fire. And after the fire came a gentle whisper.
1 KINGS 19:12

The best way to get someone's attention in a crowded room is to whisper. But in order to hear, you must tune out every extraneous noise. Sometimes it even means going somewhere quieter so you can listen.

In the same way, hearing God's gentle, reassuring whisper means turning down the volume in your life. It may mean shutting off your car stereo while you drive or taking a walk without your iPod. It may even mean quieting yourself and saying nothing at all. Then in the stillness...listen.

Our lives are bombarded with distractions and noises that drown out God's gentle whisper. Over time, we grow accustomed to the constant din of everyday commotion. In fact, we get comfortable with our distractions. But if you're stressed out and need a touch from God or you're wondering why you're struggling to sense His presence, get away from the distraction or turn down the volume so you won't miss His gentle whisper.

He's whispering to you right now. Are you listening?

Lord, I can turn down the volume in my life by...

Blessed Stillness

Be still, and know that I am God.
PSALM 46:10

Western society suffers from an acute case of Attention Deficit Disorder. Our attention spans run short, and we insist on living at breakneck speed. We work longer hours and fill our spare time with constant activity.

Our obsession with busyness points to a deeper issue. We're uncomfortable with stillness and silence. Deeper still, many of us derive our value from being productive. Our busyness, however, doesn't lend itself to connecting with God. In fact, it pushes Him to the margins of our lives.

Throughout Scripture, God calls us to slow down, to be still and say nothing at all.

Being still means yielding control; being silent means you can no longer establish the agenda. But after turning down the volume and bringing your life to a halt—at least temporarily—you now make room for God to speak to you and fill you with His life-giving presence.

So be still...and know that God is in control. Listen to the blessed silence and attune the ears of your heart to the God who longs to commune with you.

Loving Father, help me make room for You by setting aside...

OCTOBER 5

Take a Breather

God blessed the seventh day and made it holy,
because on it he rested from all the work
of creating that he had done.
GENESIS 2:3

One of the most common addictions in our society is the addiction to productivity. Our driven nature compels us to work long hours, volunteer at church or our favorite charity, and then play hard on the weekends. We want to do something. We need to do something. Anything to stay busy.

God, on the other hand, created the earth in six days and then rested on the seventh. Think about it: the God of the universe took the day off—and life continued.

Believe it or not, life will continue when you take a day off every week too. Spend it relaxing, enjoying time with family and friends, reading your Bible, journaling, praying, even sleeping. The possibilities are endless.

Benefits of taking a day of rest include a longer life, clarity of thinking, increased energy the rest of the week, and greater sensitivity to God's presence around you. Furthermore, God calls us to rest. In fact, doing nothing may be the most productive thing you do.

Heavenly Father, I commit to making time to rest by...

The Importance of Closets

*When you pray, go into your private room, shut your door,
and pray to your Father who is in secret.*
MATTHEW 6:6 HCSB

Has someone's prayer ever impressed you so much that you felt inadequate afterward? Perhaps the person's eloquence or knowledge of the Bible made your prayer seem like vague mumblings. You might be surprised to know that audacious prayers didn't impress Jesus. He even told His disciples that when they pray, they should find a remote place so they can pray to their heavenly Father in secret.

When you pray in front of others, forget about what the people around you will think. Strive to make a connection with God. He's much more interested in the passion of your heart than the eloquence of your words.

When you can, find a quiet place to pray alone where you can stay focused and listen. Without distractions, you may find yourself engaged in a real conversation. Prayer is most powerful when it is living and vital.

God, I want to connect to You through...

_____

_____

_____

_____

_____

_____

_____

Be Who You Are

They heard the sound of the Lord God walking
in the garden at the time of the evening breeze,
and the man and his wife hid themselves
from the presence of the Lord God.
GENESIS 3:8 NRSV

If you could share your deepest secrets with God without fear, what would you say? After Adam and Eve disobeyed their heavenly Father and ate the forbidden fruit, they hid themselves from His presence. Imagine trying to hide from the God of the universe!

Yet many of us follow Adam and Eve's example. We shield our mistakes from Him by refusing to acknowledge them. We conceal our emotions for fear that He will condemn us.

Every square inch of creation lies within God's full and constant view. He sees it all—including the darkest corners of your heart. But be encouraged. He loves you and accepts you regardless of the secrets that lurk within you. Open your heart and confess your faults to Him with abandon. God wants you to know the freedom that comes from being who you really are in His presence. Even now, He is waiting.

Lord God, the hidden thoughts and emotions I want to share with You are...

....

....

....

....

....

....

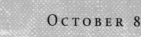

OCTOBER 8

Overcoming the Awkward Silence

No longer do I call you slaves...but I have called you friends.
JOHN 15:15 NASB

Have you ever experienced the awkward silence that occurs between two strangers in an elevator or other small space? Conversation, if it happens at all, is strained and uncomfortable. By contrast, two friends look for places where they can be alone to talk—and God considers us His friends.

When you come to God in prayer, leave the formal "thees" and "thous" behind. There is no need of pretense. Simply be who you are. Laugh, cry, even joke around. Close friends realize that they don't need to fill the air with words. Sometimes they can be together without saying anything at all.

Prayer is like a muscle. The more you use it, the stronger it becomes. In the same way, the more you dialogue with God, the easier it will become. Soon, you'll be eager to put what you're doing aside, seek out your best friend, and have a nice long talk with Him. And when you do, He'll be waiting.

Lord God, I have so much to share with You today, like...

OCTOBER 9

Prayer with an Attitude

With every prayer and request, pray at all times in the Spirit.
EPHESIANS 6:18 HCSB

Let's be realistic: Unless you live in a monastery, you can't spend all day on your knees. Life refuses to slow down, regardless of your plans or intentions. Fortunately, prayer isn't confined to a block of time. That's why it's important to know the difference between praying and being prayerful.

There will be times when you should get away for intentional, focused prayer. Your soul craves it. But that doesn't mean your prayer must come to an end when you come back to your everyday world. When you make prayer a mindset, an attitude, your prayer continues throughout the day. Being prayerful means engaging in a continuous conversation with God.

Throughout your day, invite your loving heavenly Father into your thoughts. Pray for your day as you drive to work. Ask Him for patience when you face a difficult situation. Breathe a prayer of thanksgiving when He shares a beautiful sunset with you. Tell Him you love Him as you drift off to sleep. And since you're engaged in a conversation, remember to be attentive to His soft, gentle whispers of reassuring love.

Heavenly Father, I can incorporate prayerfulness into my life even when...

Dealing with Distractions

Keep your eyes straight ahead; ignore all sideshow distractions..
PROVERBS 4:23 MSG

There will be times when your heart is heavy as you go to your quiet place with God. It's difficult to relax because your mind is spinning with tasks to accomplish, people to contact, problems to solve. So many distractions are pushing their way into your space that you can't begin to get quiet and still before Him. It's difficult to even know where to start.

When you find yourself wrestling with distractions, you might want to try praying the distractions. That means offering up to God any errant thought that might come to your mind. Try to avoid editing out anything that you might consider unimportant. Perhaps the Holy Spirit is laying an unknown need on your heart right at that moment, and if you try to ignore it, you're actually moving away from prayer that moves God's heart. Or, perhaps, praying the distraction will deliver you from worrying *about* the distraction.

Whatever the case, dealing directly with distractions is the best way to clear your heart for true communion with God.

Father God, some of the distractions I need to pray about include...

_____

_____

_____

_____

_____

_____

_____

First Comes Desire

Where your treasure is, there your heart will be also.
MATTHEW 6:21 NASB

What is your greatest desire? Perhaps you want to live a secure life or a life without pain. Or maybe you want to know God or be used by Him.

Believe it or not, that is a prayer—even if you have never verbalized the words. Augustine, the great church father, taught that prayer begins with desire, and the Bible describes some prayers as "groanings too deep for words." Your truest prayer finds itself rooted in your greatest groanings and desires.

Unfortunately, it's possible for your prayers to actually lead you away from God. When your desires become self-serving, God becomes second in importance. If you want to explore your deepest desires, take an inventory of your words, your checkbook or credit card statement, the time you spend, or the direction your thoughts gravitate to when they aren't engaged in anything specific.

The good news is that your desires can change. Your private world can be renovated and redirected. By making Jesus your greatest desire, your greatest treasure, you will receive the greatest, most satisfying gift of all: Him.

Heavenly Father, my truest, deepest desires include...

Yours to Enjoy

First we were loved, now we love. He loved us first.
1 JOHN 4:19 MSG

You were created to enjoy a satisfying relationship with God. Almost sounds too good to be true, but it is. More than a life of fun or happiness or making a difference in your world, God created you to enjoy Him.

So how do we enter this satisfying relationship with God? Begin by inviting Him into every area of your life. That might make you a little uncomfortable, but the next step makes the first step easier: Accept the fact that God is crazy about you. You are His heart's delight. That's right. The Creator of the universe deeply enjoys time spent with you. It's very hard to resist someone who cares about you like that.

When something good happens to you, thank Him for making it happen. When you're having a rough day, ask Him for strength. When you need to process your feelings, confide in Him. You don't need to set aside time to tell Him, just tell Him.

Over time, you'll discover that He *is* your deepest satisfaction.

Lord God, I can invite Your presence in my life specifically when...

Delighting in God

Take delight in the LORD, and he will give you the desires of your heart.
PSALM 37:4

Have you ever noticed that people who enjoy spending time together often act alike, even dress alike, and share similar opinions?

The same thing happens in our relationship with God. Making Him your deepest satisfaction and delight always changes you—from the inside out. His thoughts become your thoughts and His desires become your desires.

Delighting yourself in the Lord also changes the way you pray. As you delight in Him—finding your satisfaction and enjoyment in Him—your personal requests still play a role in your prayers, but your perspective on your requests will begin to resemble His. Best of all, God will grant them because they're one with His.

As we delight ourselves in the Lord, we stop going to Him only when we need something. Instead, He becomes our joy, our hope, our delight.

One-sided relationships that exist to meet our whims and desires ultimately bring little satisfaction. Relationships where both parties love, enjoy, and delight in each other, offer the greatest satisfaction—and in our relationship with God, we receive what we both desire.

Father God, I delight in You. Help me find satisfaction in...

Refocusing Your Perspective

Since we are receiving a kingdom that cannot be shaken,
let us be thankful, and so worship God acceptably with reverence and awe.
HEBREWS 12:28

The daily grind can really wear a person down. You know you're getting there when your thoughts and words become loaded with negativity and cynicism. You begin to question the motives of others and maybe even doubt God's goodness and willingness to intervene in your life.

When you feel yourself entertaining these thoughts, it's time to refocus your perspective. Imagine the difference between being stuck in a traffic jam and watching the traffic jam from the top of a mountain. Traffic jams bring out the worst in people, but observing them from a mountaintop can remind us that life is so much more than a slow-moving line of cars.

To refocus your perspective, begin by worshiping God in prayer. The most common word in the Bible for worship means "to kiss." You kiss God by telling Him how much you love Him and by showing Him reverence and respect.

Worshipping God draws your eyes off of yourself and onto the eternal God who sees you from heaven's perspective.

God, help me to refocus my worship especially when...

The Power of Praise

He hath sent me...to appoint unto them that mourn in Zion...
the garment of praise for the spirit of heaviness.
ISAIAH 61:1, 3 KJV

Do you ever feel like discouragement is sticking to you like a static-filled shirt? No matter how hard you try, you just can't shake it off. The next time you feel down, remove that old ratty shirt and exchange it for a shirt of praise.

To praise God means to acknowledge His character and works. In other words, you're telling God how great He is. Now, He already knows, but you need to say the words to remind yourself. How can you trust in God if you don't fully believe that He is able to do what He says He will do and keep His promises to you?

Begin by telling God what makes Him great. Do you enjoy early morning sunrises? Then give Him credit. Do you appreciate the air that you breathe? Give Him credit for that, too. Are you ever overwhelmed by His steadfast love for you? You know what to do.

Praise will strengthen every aspect of your relationship with God and especially your confidence that He will hear your prayers and answer them.

Lord God, my life has shown me that You deserve praise for...

God's Ultimate Purpose in Prayer

Celebrate God all day, every day.
I mean, revel in him!
PHILIPPIANS 4:4 MSG

The Bible uses different words for prayer. Some mean "to ask" or "wish," others "to address." If you were to ask the average person on the street, "Why do we pray?" you would most likely get an answer like, "Because I need a miracle."

While prayer may include asking God for a miracle, the purpose of prayer goes much deeper than your requests. The movement of God in the world is to bring glory to Himself. However, before you start leveling stones at God for being a narcissist, explore what the word "glory" means.

The word "glory" in the Bible can be translated "radiance" or "honor." But perhaps the best translation of the word is "goodness." In the Old Testament book of Exodus, Moses was discouraged and needed a touch from God. He asked God, "Show me Your glory," and God answered "I'll show you My goodness"—which He did.

The ultimate purpose of prayer is to taste the goodness of God and for other people to taste it as well. Savor it. Enjoy it. Revel in it.

Father, I can see Your goodness in...

_____

_____

_____

_____

_____

_____

The Power of Praying God's Word

If you abide in Me, and My words abide in you,
you will ask what you desire, and it shall be done for you.
JOHN 15:7 NKJV

Do you ever feel powerless in prayer? Perhaps you feel like you're talking to a wall. In order to give flight to their prayers, some people make a practice of praying verses right out of the Bible.

Of course, God would not want you to pray this way exclusively, but when it comes to pulling yourself out of a rut, what could be more powerful and inherently right than to pray God's very words? The writer of the New Testament book of Hebrews described the Bible as "living" and "active." Your Bible is so much more than ink on a page (or digital images on your computer screen). Integrating it into your prayer life is like filling your prayers with high octane gasoline.

An easy way to begin is by praying a stanza from the Old Testament book of Psalms. As you gain confidence and familiarity, call on a passage that best expresses your feelings or needs. You will soon feel your joy and confidence return.

Lord God, one verse that would empower my prayers is...

....

....

....

....

....

....

....

....

October 18

Singing the Blues

Those who have been ransomed by the Lord will return.
They will enter Jerusalem singing, crowned with everlasting joy.
Sorrow and mourning will disappear, and they will be filled with joy and gladness.
Isaiah 35:10 NLT

How do you work through your anxiety, grief, or discouragement? Rather than succumb to unhealthy habits and behaviors, it's best to have a strategy that will serve you well when unpleasant emotions come calling.

The Bible tells us that the people of ancient Israel understood the importance of acknowledging their negative emotions. Often, the people recited prayers and sang songs called laments. A lament is a song or poem that expresses anxiety, grief, discouragement, or any other negative emotion. The Bible is full of them. One book—Lamentations—is a lament in five stanzas.

Laments are actually similar to what we call singing the blues. When you're dealing with negative emotions, put what you're feeling into words and get them out in the open. Then when you're through singing the blues, begin to sing praise to God, for He is the one who can turn your sadness and frustration into joy and hope for the future.

Heavenly Father, the lament I want to sing today is about...

God's Word and Prayer

His delight is in the law of the LORD, and in His law he meditates day and night.
PSALM 1:2 NKJV

The Bible is often called God's Word because it constitutes His message to us and all mankind. For that reason, prayer and the Bible go together like seed and soil. Each one needs the other to fulfill its truest purpose.

When you water the seed of God's Word by reading it and then prayerfully pondering what it means, that is called meditation. Prayerfully reading the Bible brings life to the words on the page. Without prayer, the principles taught therein remain in your head without much chance of touching your heart. So prayer opens your eyes to how God thinks and then helps you apply it to your situation.

Praying without the principles in the Bible will leave you directionless, like embarking on a journey without a map. But understanding biblical principles and including them in your prayers will keep you headed straight on to victory. Your prayers are sure to be powerful when they are coupled with God's words.

Father God, I would like to strengthen the power of the Bible in my life by...

Calling for Help

He will deliver the needy who cry out,
the afflicted who have no one to help.
PSALM 72:12

Imagine that you and a friend are separated from each other while attending a parade. The battery on your cell phone is dead, which means you can't even find your friend's phone number on your phone to make a call from someone else's phone. So you begin calling out your friend's name. Finally, you hear your friend call out your name as well. Slowly, the two of you inch your way back to each other.

Throughout the New Testament, we're told that when we call on the name of Jesus, He shows up. Granted, He's always present (He's God!), but when we call on His name, He shows up in a special way. Like being lost in a crowd, calling on the name of Jesus guides us closer to Him.

When you're in trouble or afraid or confused, call on Jesus by name. The Bible says the name of Jesus is powerful and influential, and He has promised to be there to help you when you call on Him.

Lord Jesus, I need Your help with...

Why Prayer Comes Naturally

The Lord has heard my supplication; the Lord accepts my prayer.
PSALM 6:9 NRSV

You were created to enjoy an unhindered relationship with God. Consider Adam and Eve. When God created and then placed them in the Garden of Eden, they communed together without any barriers. God designed them to enjoy a mutually interactive relationship with Him. And, because you are a direct descendent of Adam and Eve, you were also created with the same inclination for divine communication, which we know as prayer.

God cares about you and desires to commune with you so much that He wired you to communicate with Him. Prayer, then, comes naturally, just like eating or breathing. It's part of your spiritual DNA.

Rather than working harder on your prayer life, let it flow naturally out of your everyday rhythms. It's more a matter of including God in your routine than partitioning a piece of your day for concerted prayer. When you awaken in the morning, envision your heavenly Father welcoming you into the new day. While you're running errands or going to work, remember that He's right beside you.

Now share the rest of your day together!

Dear Father, I want to share with You about...

When Life Is Good

*Far be it from me that I should sin against
the LORD by ceasing to pray for you.*
1 SAMUEL 12:23 NASB

Many people cry out to God in desperate times. When times are good? Not so much. While reaching for God in our hardship is always beneficial, maintaining the same mindset during prosperous times is equally important. The approach, however, may be different.

In times of difficulty, we tend to ask God to intervene in our lives, so our prayers take the form of a request. When we experience those all-too-rare moments when problems seem like a distant memory, our prayers can take the form of thanksgiving. Granted, requests and thanksgiving aren't mutually exclusive, but prayer is often dominated by one or the other.

Keeping the communication lines open with God when life is good is a reminder that you need Him. Always. God is your provider, encourager, and the giver of life. Without Him you would have nothing and be nothing. And thanking Him in seasons of abundance helps you remember that. Ultimately, it reminds you that you're not alone. Everything good in your life comes directly from your loving heavenly Father.

Lord God, thank You for blessing me with...

Overcoming Your Doubts

What if some were unfaithful? Will their unfaithfulness nullify God's faithfulness? Not at all!
ROMANS 3:3–4

When you're praying, do you ever think that it won't make a difference? That's probably the most common reason people stop praying. You may have felt that way in the past. You may even feel that way right now.

If you struggle with doubt, then try this: Pray your doubts. It certainly does no good to hide them from God. He already knows you have them. Instead, voice them loud and clear. Name every one and describe how you feel in detail. Tell Him why you doubt His goodness, His power, His love...perhaps even His existence. Doubt can hurt you only when it is harbored, cloaked in darkness as it were. As long as it remains hidden, it can't be examined and dealt with.

But did you ever consider that doubt is necessary in order to have faith? If you had no doubts, you wouldn't need any faith, and you wouldn't need to pray. Practically speaking, prayer and doubt are all but inseparable. Your doubts let you know where you need to shore up your faith.

Lord God, the doubts that keep me from praying confidently are...

Does God Answer Prayer?

Call to me and I will answer you, and will tell you great and hidden things that you have not known.
JEREMIAH 33:3 NRSV

Does God answer our prayers? The short answer to the question is yes—He always answers. The long answer is He doesn't always answer in the way we expect Him to.

God's answers to our requests usually fall into one of three categories: yes, no, and wait awhile. When He answers yes, we often respond by crediting Him for His faithfulness. When He answers no, we're tempted to question His goodness, wisdom, or power. But think about it: Isn't it good that God doesn't always align Himself with our will? His wisdom and perspective are so much greater than ours. If God always answered our requests in the way we think best, the world would be in utter chaos.

The most difficult answer might be to wait awhile. It means persevering in prayer in spite of what we can see. "Wait awhile" might look like a no, but it requires that we patiently continue in faith. Special treasures await those who through faith and perseverance wait on God. He always answers prayer.

Lord God, I know that You hear and answer my prayers because...

When God Says "Wait"

*Do not lose the courage you had in the past,
which has a great reward. You must hold on, so you can do
what God wants and receive what he has promised.*

Hebrews 10:35–36 NCV

Persevering in prayer isn't for the fainthearted. Anyone can offer a quick prayer to God for a pressing need. But continuing to bring that need to God over time requires uncommon faith.

Nothing pleases God more than faith—and sometimes faith simply means holding on. The truest picture of faith isn't receiving an affirmative answer to your request—it's holding on when everything in your world urges you to quit.

By refusing to give up, you're actually growing stronger day by day. Author E. M. Bounds once wrote, "Prayer in its highest form and grandest success assumes the attitude of a wrestler with God. It is the contest, trial, and victory of faith; a victory not secured from an enemy, but from Him who tries our faith that He may enlarge it; that tests our strength to make us stronger."

If you're tempted to let go of an earnest request, don't give up! Hold on until you see the answer!

Lord God, I'm waiting for Your answer to my prayer for...

OCTOBER 26

When God Says No

We can be so sure that every detail in our lives of love for God is worked into something good.
ROMANS 8:28 MSG

Probably the most unpopular word in the English language is "no." Adults don't want to hear it from kids, and kids don't want to hear it from adults.

At least parents understand the importance of the word. "No" is the word you need when it comes to playing ball in the street at night, eating paint, or riding a skateboard being pulled behind a car. Parents inherently understand that "no" doesn't mean "I don't love you." Actually, a "no" can mean "I *do* love you."

If you're a child of God, the same truth applies. When God says no to your requests, it doesn't mean He doesn't love you. Coping with the no, however, may be painful. An ongoing sickness or disease is difficult to endure. Extended unemployment can throw your life into chaos.

When God's no doesn't make sense to you, trust the heart of your Father in heaven. Your best interests are always on His heart. You can trust Him even when you don't understand. He's a good parent.

Heavenly Father, when my prayers are answered with a no, I feel...

A Framework, Not a Formula

Pray like this.
MATTHEW 6:9 NLT

When Jesus' disciples asked Him to teach them about prayer, He gave them a solid model to go by. Nowadays, this model prayer is commonly known as the Lord's Prayer.

The Lord's Prayer begins by focusing our attention on God's holiness. What good would it do to pray if we are not sure we can trust the one we are praying to? Next, we get some much-needed perspective when our attention is drawn to the bigger picture—God's kingdom and His will, established in heaven. From there we find assurance that we can bring our needs to Him, ask for and receive forgiveness, and find the courage to stand strong against temptation. Finally, we acknowledge the greatness of our God, settling in our hearts that God is solidly in charge, able to handle all we might bring to Him.

The Lord's Prayer is a framework rather than a formula—a starting point for your prayers. It allows you to better understand what God feels is important in your relationship with Him. What a wonderful God He is, for He not only invites us to pray but shows us how.

Lord in heaven, my needs today are...

Fellowship with God

Our fellowship is with the Father and with his Son, Jesus Christ.
1 JOHN 1:3

Did you know God created you for deep fellowship with Him? More than your requests for forgiveness or your appeals for a better life, God wants you. He wants to commune with *you*.

The Bible tells us that we are created in the image of God. That means in the deepest places of our being, we're just like Him. So *how* are we like Him? Our God is a relational God. The Father, Son, and Holy Spirit, whom we know as the Trinity, commune with one another in a relationship of love.

Out of their relationship of loving intimacy, out of their desire to share their love, they created Adam and Eve. And as a direct descendent of creation's first couple, you were created in the image of our relational God with the intention that you would be in sweet fellowship with Him.

That fellowship finds its place in prayer—conversing with Him day after day. What an amazing opportunity, privilege, and blessing such fellowship provides. Open your heart to it, one day at a time.

Father God, fellowship with You means...

First Line of Defense

Because he himself suffered when he was tempted, he is able to help those who are being tempted.
HEBREWS 2:18

Twenty-five percent of the Netherlands, a country situated in the northwest corner of Europe, lies below sea level. Centuries ago, its people constructed dikes in order to prevent flooding and to reclaim the land. Their system of dikes acts as a first line of defense against the ocean.

In the same way, all of us live below sea level in regard to temptation. Without any line of defense, all of us are subject to temptation's persistent onslaught. Prayer acts as a dike that prevents temptation from flooding into every area of our lives.

Even Jesus needed to strengthen his dike. He fasted and prayed in the wilderness for forty days in order to withstand the alluring propositions of his enemy, Satan. Jesus understood that prayer strengthens our souls, because our spirit may be willing, but our flesh is indeed weak. So repeatedly throughout the four Gospels, He cautioned his followers to watch and pray.

Ask God to show you the areas of weakness in your dike and give you strength to withstand the waves of temptation that beat against you.

Lord God, I feel my dike needs to be strengthened in the area of...

Forget the Past

I let it all out; I said,
"I'll make a clean breast of my failures to GOD."
Suddenly the pressure was gone—my guilt dissolved, my sin disappeared.
PSALM 32:5 MSG

Prayer not only serves as our principle form of communication with God, it also functions as a barometer of our soul's health. Whenever we feel reluctant to pray, something is amiss.

Oftentimes our past operates as our biggest deterrent to pray. When we're ashamed of our misdeeds or afraid of God's anger, we tend to avoid Him. The good news is this: God has done everything in His power to restore your relationship with Him. You cannot do anything to earn His forgiveness because He offers it freely to you. All you must do is acknowledge to Him your regret, and He will wipe away any barrier between the two of you.

Best of all, God will never remind you of your past embarrassments. He is overwhelmed with love for you and longs for you to enjoy an unhindered relationship with Him. God's relentless love and acceptance is reason enough to bring Him all your guilt and regrets. Go ahead. Take the first step. He's waiting.

Father God, today I commit my regrets to You, specifically...

....

....

....

....

....

....

....

Power in the Name of Jesus

At the name of Jesus every knee should bend, in heaven and on earth and under the earth.
PHILIPPIANS 2:10–11 NRSV

No other name in heaven and earth exerts power over darkness and evil like the name of Jesus. Scripture tells us that at the *name* of Jesus every knee will bow and every tongue confess that Jesus Christ is the supreme power.

While at its core prayer is our conversation with God, prayer can also be your primary weapon in the ongoing conflict with dark powers. Evil exists, and fueling the evil in this world is the prince of darkness, Satan. From him flows all deceit, fear, greed, and every wicked thing. On our own, we're powerless over our formidable foe. But thanks be to God, we do not fight alone!

If you struggle with nightmares or fear, come against them with the name of Jesus. Just say, "In the name of Jesus, I refuse to be overcome by fear." Or invite Jesus *by name* to intervene in your situation.

You cannot win your battles on your own. But Jesus can fight them for you, and He always wins. So invite Him right now into the dark places of your life.

Jesus, I call on Your name to intervene in my life for...

Your Biggest Cheering Section

*Let us run the race that is
before us and never give up.*
HEBREWS 12:1 NCV

Imagine yourself running a marathon through the streets of a great city. You followed your training program, but nevertheless, the race has required every last ounce of strength. As you near the end, you enter the stadium where you will run one lap to finish the trek. You're unsure whether you can make it to the tape. You wobble past the entrance and enter the track. Suddenly you hear a loud noise. The spectators in the crowd are cheering you on, encouraging you to finish strong. Like a charge of electricity coursing through your veins, you find new strength to make it to the end.

You are not alone. You've been given the Father, Son, and Holy Spirit to guide and strengthen you every day. But the saints in heaven are cheering you on, as well. The Bible tells us that we are surrounded by a great cloud of witnesses. They are the people who ran before you and finished strong.

On this day—All Saints Day—we remember the great saints of the past. But this year, don't just remember them. Listen. They're cheering you on.

Heavenly Father, I want to hear the encouragement of the saints regarding...

....

....

....

....

....

....

....

The Shameless Request

In the morning, LORD, you hear my voice; in the morning
I lay my requests before you and wait expectantly.
PSALM 5:3

In the Bible, we read about King Hezekiah, who had reigned over the southern kingdom of Judah with godliness and integrity. Under his solid leadership, he brought stability and spiritual reform to his people. But now his life was coming to a premature end at the age of thirty-nine. His illness was so pronounced that people had already begun to say their goodbyes.

Hezekiah, though, wasn't ready to go. "Please, Lord. Let me live," he cried out.

All of us face moments in our lives when we face a nearly insurmountable problem. A dismal prognosis from a doctor. A marriage that's barely holding it together. Financial collapse. By all appearances, the death certificate has been signed, sealed, and delivered. Asking God to rescue us seems so...so shameless.

Not so fast. No request is too big for God because God is always greater than your greatest need. While He doesn't say yes to every request, He did for Hezekiah—and gave him another fifteen years to live.

Be bold and ask the shameless request.

Lord God, I have a few shameless requests to make, including...

God and the Small Stuff

Do not be anxious about anything, but in every situation,
by prayer and petition, with thanksgiving, present your requests to God.
PHILIPPIANS 4:6

Do you ever wonder if God is interested in the small stuff? Is He too busy dealing with world affairs to be concerned with the insignificant details of your life?

Charles Spurgeon, the great nineteenth-century preacher, once said, "Whether we like it or not, asking is the rule of the kingdom." Repeatedly in the Bible, we're encouraged to bring *all* of our requests to God, no matter how big or small. We're told to bring anything and everything to God. That pretty much covers it!

No request, emotion, or infirmity is too small in God's eyes.

All too often, we don't see God intervene in the small stuff because we haven't invited Him to do so. We don't receive the answers to our requests because we haven't asked Him. But God loves *you*—not just the mass of humanity. He sent His Son Jesus to die for *you*. And He hears every prayer, no matter how big or how seemingly small.

So throw caution to the wind and invite God into your small stuff!

Heavenly Father, help me with the small stuff of life, like...

Praying in the Moment

Let each of you look not to your own interests, but to the interests of others.
PHILIPPIANS 2:4 NRSV

Have friends or acquaintances ever asked you to pray for some need in their lives—maybe a sickness or financial problem? You said yes, but realistically, you didn't know how to pray for that person—or once away from the situation you just forgot to do it.

If this has happened to you, you aren't alone. That's why it's important to learn to pray in the moment. Instead of entrusting another person's request to memory, you might offer to pray with that person right then. If that feels too awkward, whisper a prayer on your own as soon as you have an opportunity.

Either way, it doesn't have to be a long, drawn-out prayer, nor do you need a private area to bring your requests to God. And don't worry, even if someone sees or hears you. The important thing is that praying in the moment ensures you'll honor your commitment, embeds the person's request in your memory, and helps you make prayer a consistent part of your lifestyle.

Father, I pray to You in this moment about...

Good Intentions

I will pray to the Lord, and he will answer me from his holy mountain.
PSALM 3:4 NCV

Imagine that you have an unemployed friend. One day you call him to find out how he's doing. "I'm working really hard at finding a job," he tells you. "This week I read two books on effective interviewing, and I ran across a helpful newspaper article on the current job market. Then I spent time on a website that highlights job openings in my particular field!" "That's great," you reply. "And how many resumés were you able to send out?" "Actually," he admits. "I didn't send any." Few people find jobs when they do everything *but* apply.

In the same way, reading books about prayer, listening to speakers teaching about prayer—all good. But sometimes, in our flurry of activity surrounding prayer, we convince ourselves that we're spending time with God when we're not. Nothing can substitute for sincere, face-to-face prayer.

If you find yourself in this position, don't beat yourself up. God's invitation to commune with Him still stands. Just close your books, turn off your media, and let God's warm embrace envelope you.

Father, forgive me for not spending time with You. Help me to…

....

....

....

....

....

....

....

Grunts and Groans

Those who love me, I will deliver; I will protect those who know my name.
When they call to me, I will answer them.
PSALM 91:14–15 NRSV

Sometimes listening to other people pray can be intimidating. Perhaps their knowledge of the Bible or their insights into God's ways can leave you feeling like a infant in regard to prayer.

From God's perspective, however, the state of your heart and the extent to which you engage with Him as you bring your requests before Him carry the greatest importance. The gut-wrenching, heartfelt prayer, replete with poor syntax, stumbling words, and simple thoughts may mean more to God than a beautifully articulated prayer. And in the places where your prayers fall short, the Bible says the Holy Spirit prays on your behalf with groans that words cannot express.

Prayer that ascends to the heavens and reaches the throne room of God is more heart than head. You don't need to be a great public speaker to pray. You don't need a strong command of the Bible. You don't need a commanding presence.

You just need to pray—even if it's a grunt or a groan.

Dear Father, what I've been trying to say to You is...

Quality Time with the Father

*God has sent the Spirit of his Son into
our hearts, crying, "Abba! Father!"*
GALATIANS 4:6 NRSV

The religious leaders of Jesus' day were irritated and unnerved by His relationship with God. He constantly called Him "Father." Now, that may not be a big deal to you, but back in the day, the religious leaders considered it an affront to treat God with such familiarity. They wouldn't even utter aloud the most intimate name for God—Yahweh—preferring to use the name Adonai instead. But "Father" was far more intimate. In one instance, Jesus even called Him "Abba," which means "Daddy."

When you come to God in prayer, you're not addressing some divine "sir." You're coming before your heavenly *Father*, and He is everything you ever dreamed a father could be. He loves you deeply and always welcomes you into His presence.

The religious leaders of Jesus' day missed out because they chose to know God only as a powerful deity. They ignored the tender father heart of God. He invites you to know Him as Jesus did. As you go to Him in prayer, open your heart to know Him deeply, fully, and affectionately.

Heavenly Father, there are so many things I love about You, like...

Your Father in Heaven

*See what love the Father has given us, that we should
be called children of God; and that is what we are.*

1 JOHN 3:1 NRSV

Every child wants to believe their dad is strong. If they grew up with one, they want to know that their father can fend for himself and defend the family. A strong father imparts to his children a sense of security, peace, and self-confidence. That's why little boys challenge other boys that "My daddy is bigger than your daddy."

During his time on earth, Jesus consistently referred to God as His Father. Neither His followers nor detractors were accustomed to considering God in such terms. But perhaps Jesus' strong sense of self partly resulted from knowing His daddy was bigger than anyone else's daddy.

And the same is true for you. Regardless of whether or not you grew up with an earthly father, you are the child of a heavenly Father who is bigger, stronger, faster, and smarter than any other daddy in the world. When you pray, remember that He's your Father in heaven, and all power in heaven and on earth lies at His disposal.

Father God, I'm glad to be Your child because...

_____

_____

_____

_____

_____

_____

_____

Your Father's Love

*Long before he laid down earth's foundations,
he had us in mind, had settled on us as the focus of his love,
to be made whole and holy by his love.*
EPHESIANS 1:4–5 MSG

One of the happiest moments in the lives of most parents is the birth of their children. The immediate and overwhelming affection parents feel for their newborns cannot be exaggerated. And, in most cases, that love continues throughout their lives. No matter what their children do—even in a child's moody, rebellious teenage years—parental love remains strong.

When you pray to your heavenly Father, you are crawling onto the lap of the one who loves you with an everlasting love. Your heavenly Father's affection for you cannot be exaggerated. You can confess your shortcomings to Him, knowing that you can do nothing to make Him love you less. You can confide in Him your greatest accomplishments, knowing you can do nothing to make Him love you more. Your Father loves you simply because you're His child. He knows and accepts you.

So when you pray, simply tell Him what you need. You are safe in His presence.

Heavenly Father, I feel safe in Your presence when...

Unlimited Access

Through Him we both have access by one Spirit to the Father.
EPHESIANS 2:18 HCSB

Imagine that your father is a powerful king. Dignitaries from around the world must receive permission to meet with him. When they arrive from their distant lands, they often must wait in line before being ushered into his presence.

But not you. He has instructed his servants to give you unlimited access into his presence. You often walk past the lines of impatient people and open the door to the throne room—without even knocking. Such are the privileges of being a child of the King of kings.

And such are the privileges at your disposal today. When you give your heart to God and avail yourself of the sacrifice Jesus made for you, you are born again into the family of God. God is your father and Jesus becomes your brother. You have all the privileges of the royal court. You don't need to clean up first or wait in line to see Him. Anytime you need Him, anytime the thought occurs to you, you can walk right in and present yourself to your Father.

Heavenly Father, I love being with You especially when...

You're Not an Only Child

The LORD is close to all who call on him, yes, to all who call on him in truth.
PSALM 145:18 NLT

When bringing requests to God, many people tend to pray only from their point of view. For example, if you're unemployed and you just interviewed for your dream job, how do you pray? Asking God to give you the job is understandable. But what about the other applicants interviewing for the same position? Should you be given the job over someone else?

When Jesus taught His disciples to pray, He instructed them to begin by saying "Our Father." You are not an only child—your Father's love extends beyond you to the people around you.

So boldly ask anything of God, remembering that sometimes His no to your request might be a yes to someone else's. Yet you can be confident in this: Your heavenly Father loves you, cares about you, and knows what He's doing as He directs the affairs of your life. For this reason, you can trust Him—regardless of the outcome.

Heavenly Father, my perspective has changed about...

....

....

....

....

....

....

....

Exercising Your Prayer Muscles

Pray without ceasing.
1 THESSALONIANS 5:17 NKJV

Not everyone can perform a violin concerto with a symphony orchestra. Nor can everyone play professional basketball or paint a beautiful landscape. Unique gifts and skills are required to participate in certain activities.

Not so with prayer.

Anyone can pray, regardless of gender, skill, or stature. The only requirements are commitment and consistency. Think about it: You can become a woman or man of prayer. Rather than a gift that is on display, prayer is like a muscle that is exercised. The more you pray, the more natural it feels and the stronger you become. The less you pray, the more unnatural it feels and the weaker you become.

Well-toned prayer muscles work all the time. While prayerful people may schedule blocks in their schedule for one-on-one time with God, their daily lives literally become a prayer. During a free moment in their schedule, they enjoy a quick God-directed conversation. When they drive by a car accident, they whisper a short request. And all of this occurs without much forethought.

And it all begins with a simple, spiritual workout that anyone can do.

God, I will better exercise my prayer muscles by...

Hearing God in Your Pain

He has not despised or scorned the suffering
of the afflicted one; he has not hidden his face
from him but has listened to his cry for help.
PSALM 22:24

Physical and emotional pain undoubtedly drives more people to pray than anything else. Ironically, nothing drives people away from God more than pain. Our afflictions bring our deepest beliefs into question.

C. S. Lewis wrote, "God whispers to us in our pleasures, speaks in our conscience, but shouts in our pains: it is His megaphone to rouse a deaf world."

Where do you go with your pain? Do you curse it and blame God? Or do you allow it to drive you deeper in your relationship with Him?

When you feel the sharp edge of pain, cry out to God. But also pay attention to His megaphone. He may not be the cause of your suffering, but He is surely speaking to you through it. Before reaching for the closest source of immediate relief, consider releasing your pain to God and listening to hear what He is saying.

Father, I think You might be trying to tell me...

Finding God in Your Pain

Just as we share abundantly in the sufferings of Christ, so also our comfort abounds through Christ.
2 CORINTHIANS 1:5

"God doesn't understand my pain. How could He when He's God?"

A common misconception is that God cannot understand our pain because He can use His powers to avoid it. How could He know the sharp sting of betrayal or the blow to the gut that results from disappointment? He's never felt the pain of injury or illness. Nor has He grieved the death of a child. But wait a minute—in fact, He has.

Because He created each one of us with a free will, He has suffered the rejection of millions who have refused His love and concern. Jesus, God's only begotten Son, came willingly to serve as a vessel of reconciliation. And yet He was cursed, beaten, abused, and unjustly executed in the most painful way imaginable.

God knows what it is like to suffer, to be misunderstood and falsely accused. He knows the pain of loss, and yet He continues to love and care and comfort. When you turn to Him in prayer, He will lift your heart and give you hope.

Heavenly Father, the things that bring me pain are...

....

....

....

....

....

....

....

Pray for Me?

*The prayer of a person living right with God
is something powerful to be reckoned with.*
JAMES 5:16 MSG

"Will you pray for me?" a friend confides to you. "Sure," you stammer. "How can I pray?"

"The doctor just told me I have cancer. I'm so afraid. I want you to pray that God will heal me." Immediately you gulp—and hopefully your friend didn't hear it. *I don't know if my friend will be healed*, you think to yourself. What do you do?

It's true: You don't know how your prayers will be answered. But God does. In His infinite love, He chooses to use us to touch other people at times. He doesn't heal every time, but nothing is impossible with God.

When praying for someone, make sure you first understand the person's request. Then as you pray, give thanks to God for His great love. Most importantly, present the need as a request on your part rather than an obligation on God's part. Then leave the results to God.

Praying for others may seem intimidating at first, but you will soon find that it can be a great blessing to help another person connect with God.

God, when someone asks me to pray I feel...

When God Doesn't Heal

Trust the Lord with all your heart, and don't depend on your own understanding.
PROVERBS 3:5 NCV

Have you ever asked God to heal you—and He didn't? Perhaps your prayer was for someone else, and God seemed to do nothing. He was silent. While God can and does heal, remember that He doesn't always answer our requests with a yes. No formula exists that obligates God to do anything. That's what makes Him God.

Jesus once healed a disabled man—but He walked through a crowd of other sick and diseased people to reach him. For some reason, God chose to restore to health one man out of the many. Why? We don't know. Paul the apostle, whom God used to heal many people, prayed for healing from a physical or emotional problem, but God chose to leave him as he was.

God invites you to come to Him with your requests—big and small. He says He will always hear you. But like any good father, His answer is not always what you might want it to be and the reason may be above your understanding. That's when you must trust Him.

Father God, I trust You concerning...

In the Midst of Sickness

May the God of hope fill you with all joy and peace as you trust in him.
ROMANS 15:13

From our perspective, ongoing sickness doesn't make a great deal of sense. How on earth can pain and suffering be good? Equally frustrating can be our continuous pleas to God for relief while He seems to do nothing.

Some of the godliest people in the Bible suffered prolonged sickness or disease. Job lost his children to tragic deaths, his belongings were destroyed, and he was stricken with painful sores all over his body. Yet the Bible tells us that God considered him "blameless and upright." A young pastor named Timothy suffered from frequent stomach problems, yet to our knowledge he never experienced relief from the pain.

This tells us that we cannot make a direct correlation between godliness and sickness. We must make peace with the fact that godly people suffer.

Never draw back from asking God to heal you. But as you bring your request, ask also that your eyes be opened to His goodness, and then trust that He is indeed doing something good in you.

God, open my eyes to see Your goodness in the midst of...

....

....

....

....

....

....

....

Inviting Jesus into Your Prayer

Believing-prayer will heal you, and Jesus will put you on your feet.
JAMES 5:15 MSG

Asking a friend or a group of people to pray for a particular need in your life requires humility. It's the acknowledgement that you have a problem that you are unable to handle on your own. Voicing it can be scary because you make yourself vulnerable to other people and give up control concerning some potentially personal information.

On the other hand, inviting others to pray for you is like increasing the voltage of your request. The power is multiplied by the number of people praying. That in itself is reason enough to ask for prayer support—but there is more. Jesus becomes present in your prayers. Jesus said that when two or three people gather in His name, He is there. He is always with you, yet somehow, in some way, His presence becomes even more evident. Gathering even two or three people in the name of Jesus to pray increases the power of your prayer exponentially.

Invite Jesus into the middle of your prayers by opening yourself to others.

Lord God, help me to invite others to pray for...

Fortified Faith

*If you have faith the size of a mustard seed, you will say to this mountain,
"Move from here to there," and it will move; and nothing will be impossible for you.*
MATTHEW 17:20–21 NRSV

A story is recorded in the Bible of a young man tormented by seizures which surfaced at the most inopportune times. The young man's father was overwhelmed with sorrow. He wanted to see his son healed, but he didn't have the faith to believe that Jesus could change his son's condition. When Jesus told him that anything is possible to those who believe, the man said that he wanted to believe and asked Jesus to help him with his doubts.

Do you ever feel overwhelmed with a problem and you lack the faith to believe that God can change it? You aren't alone. The answer is to be honest with God. Ask Him to strengthen and fortify your faith and help you deal with your doubts.

That's what this caring father did, and it made a difference for the young man plagued with seizures. It can make a difference for you as well.

God, I want to deal with my doubts. They are...

Go Ahead and Ask

With God's power working in us, God can do much,
much more than anything we can ask or imagine.
EPHESIANS 3:20 NCV

In the 1968 Academy Award-winning movie *Oliver!*, Oliver Twist, a young orphan, asks the cantankerous Mr. Bumble for a second helping of gruel. "What?" the workhouse director asks. "Please sir, I want some more?" Chaos erupts as Bumble and his cohorts chase Oliver Twist in hopes of punishing him.

Addressing the Almighty might evoke similar scenarios in your head. What right do we have to ask anything of God beyond our daily necessities? And what will He do if we say something that's offensive or selfish?

The good news about God is that He's better than you ever imagined. The Bible tells us that God is able to surpass your wildest, most far-fetched prayers, desires, hopes, or requests. If you ask wrongly or selfishly, that's okay. He'll let you know. If you ask for something that He considers frivolous or unnecessary, don't sweat it. He won't punish you for praying incorrectly. He doesn't promise to always say yes, but He does promise that you won't be chastised for asking.

God, I've been meaning to ask about...

God Is for You

"I know the plans I have for you," declares the LORD,
"plans to prosper you and not to harm you, plans to give you hope and a future."
JEREMIAH 29:11

If you want to discover what you really believe about your heavenly Father, look at how you relate to Him. If your communication with Him is hit or miss, you're likely to perceive Him as an easily distracted father. If you avoid Him and feel guilty when you bring Him your requests, you probably see Him as a begrudging, cantankerous father who doesn't care. If you cower when you're addressing Him, then you probably view Him as cold or unforgiving. Such caricatures of God, though, are inaccurate.

God is on your side. Think about that for a moment. God is more for you than you are for yourself. He cares about you. God will only work good in your life. For this reason, you can confide in Him, you can confess to Him, and you can come to Him any time, without guilt, fear, or apology. God is for *you*!

And if God is for you, you need nothing else.

God, please free me from my misconceptions of You including...

....

....

....

....

....

....

....

The God Who Sings

[God] will rejoice over you with singing.
ZEPHANIAH 3:17

When holding a newborn in their arms, proud parents and grandparents coo like a baby, talk like a baby, and regardless of their degree of musical ability, they sing. Proud parents and grandparents have few inhibitions.

Did you know that God feels the same way about you—even in your old age? The Bible says He delights in you. That means when He thinks of you, He is overcome with joy. He is so overwhelmed with love for you that He sings over you, just like a loving father unabashedly sings over his child. God's truest desires are unrestrained where His children are concerned.

Think about the song He is singing over you. Listen for it when you are in quiet prayer, waiting in His presence. It's a song that brings you peace in the midst of distress. It's a song filled with warm affection. It's a song describing the joy He feels when He calls you His own. Listen to it. Believe in it. It is your song; a song He wrote for you alone.

Lord God, when I hear a whisper of Your song over me, I will...

Thanks-living

Give thanks in all circumstances for this is
God's will for you in Christ Jesus.
1 THESSALONIANS 5:18

Hold your breath for a moment. Now exhale. Inhale again. Exhale. Isn't it amazing that you can inhale and exhale at will, yet when you aren't thinking about it, your body breathes on its own? Now try making your heart stop beating. Fortunately, God designed your heart to work apart from your attempts to control it. Every breath you take, every beat your heart makes, is a gift from God.

You live in a constant downpour of God's generous love. Some of His amazing gifts can be identified quite easily, but most require some thought and reflection. During this Thanksgiving season, consider taking time to begin a list of the many things you can be thankful for. The first dozen items will probably come easily. But the longer you work at it, the more difficult it will become. Your efforts, however, will guide you into new frontiers of God's boundless wisdom and never-ending love.

Spend time thanking Him for the many gifts He has given you, without asking anything in return.

Dear God, I'm thankful for...

Your Life Is a Prayer

Devote yourselves to prayer with an alert mind and a thankful heart.
COLOSSIANS 4:2 NLT

If a picture is worth a thousand words, a life must be worth millions. A former president of Princeton University once said, "As a young man, I accepted Christ and the gift of eternal life. All the rest of my life was simply a P.S. to that day, saying, 'Thank You, Lord, for what you gave to me then.'"

If your life is a prayer of thanksgiving to God, what are you praying? Your everyday actions reveal your truest values and intentions. When you give, you acknowledge that God has given you far more than you could ever repay. When you forgive, you acknowledge that through Christ, you have been forgiven far more than you deserve. When you direct credit or praise toward your heavenly Father, you acknowledge that everything good in your life comes from Him.

During this Thanksgiving season, take time to evaluate what your life is praying. If it doesn't line up with the desires God has given you, remember the many ways He has blessed you— and then live your prayer.

Father, I'd like my life to be a prayer of thanks to You. Thank You for...

The Prayer that Never Ends

I bless the Lord who gives me counsel;
in the night also my heart instructs me.
I keep the LORD always before me.
PSALM 16:7–8 NRSV

Most people bring their prayer to a close by saying "amen." The word appears a hundred and fifty-one times in the Bible, and refers, to varying degrees, to telling the truth. In connection with prayer, people in the Bible used the word to mean "Let it be true," or "Let it be so."

When we say amen in prayer, many of us act like our conversation with God has come to an end, so we move on with our day. Kind of like saying, "See you later." But what if you prayed and then intentionally chose not to say amen?

Without an amen, you'll likely be much more aware of God's presence with you throughout the day. Best of all, you may feel greater freedom to continue your conversation with Him. You can silently ask Him for wisdom during a meeting. Laugh together about some humorous situation. Or thank Him for the pasta recipe you discovered on the Internet.

Isn't it amazing what a difference a little word makes?

Father, let my life be a continual prayer even when...

....

....

....

....

....

....

....

Walking with God

*Enoch walked faithfully with God;
then he was no more, because God took him away.*
GENESIS 5:24

When we walk with God over a lifetime, something changes inside us. The Bible describes a man named Enoch, who walked with God. One day while the two were enjoying their walk, God took him away (presumably to heaven). Some people imagine that Enoch and God walked so far that God glanced at his walking partner and said, "Hey Enoch, we're closer to my home than yours, why don't you just stay with me?" And Enoch accepted God's invitation.

A lifetime of walking with God is a little like that.

Enoch surely faced many opportunities to make sinful choices—and he stumbled quite a few times. But something must have shifted in Enoch's heart over the years as the result of constant communion with God: heaven became much more familiar than earth.

God would like your whole life to be a prayer—one long conversation so to speak. Once that happens, your perspective changes. Heavenly things will become your priority and your life here on earth will likely be changed forever.

Dear God, some of the things I love about walking with You are...

....

....

....

....

....

....

....

Give and Take

Here I am! I stand at the door and knock. If anyone hears my voice and opens the door,
I will come in and eat with that person, and they with me.
REVELATION 3:20

There are many ingredients to a healthy relationship: laughter, shared interests, and obviously, love. And of course, there is the give-and-take component. In other words, a healthy relationship is always a two-way street.

The same applies to our relationship with God.

While God joyfully listens to our requests, He desires so much more than a one-sided relationship. He relishes moments when you offer to be an extension of His love in your world. He longs for you to enjoy Him for who He is as much as for what He can do for you. And He feels right at home being with you, even when you ask nothing of Him at all.

What kind of relationship do you have with God? Do you see Him only as someone you bring your requests to? God wants a give-and-take relationship with you, a two-way conversation. Will you open your heart to true relationship with Him?

Father, I want to have a real conversation with You about...

Worshiping the Creator

Ascribe to the LORD the glory due his name;
worship the LORD in the splendor of his holiness.
PSALM 29:2

Morning walks can be invigorating. The coolness of the fresh air gently blowing across your face, the subtle yet distinctive smells, and the varied offerings of scenic views can awaken even the most sluggish senses.

They also contribute to an ideal environment for prayer.

While Jesus explained the benefits of praying in a closet, walking and praying can refresh your prayer life too. The sound of birds singing or the vision of an ever-changing sunrise naturally leads to worship. It's easy, though, to ignore the obvious reminders of a creative God who reveals Himself through His creation. You don't even need to get away from the city to find inspiration for worship. Have you ever considered the intricacies of a car parked along the road? It took some real creativity to build it—an example of the intelligence and insight God has shared with us.

Everywhere you go, everything you see points to the all-wise God who loves you and shares Himself with you. And the most natural response is to pray and worship.

God, I see Your creativity all around in...

The Neighborly Way

Love your neighbor as you love yourself.
LEVITICUS 19:18 NCV

God loves your neighbor every bit as much as He loves you. And He calls *you* to love your neighbor as well. Jesus said that the greatest commandment is to love God with all that is in you and to love your neighbor as yourself. Some neighbors you know, but how do you love those neighbors you don't know?

Begin by praying for them.

As you pray, God will help you see them through His eyes. Resentments and irritation will melt away as God's compassion flows to you and through you. Ask your heavenly Father to meet their needs—though you may not know what those needs are. Pray that they would draw closer to God and reach out for His presence in their lives.

Your prayers don't have to be fancy or detailed. God is able to look beyond your words and see your heart. He may also choose to use you to answer some aspects of your prayers. Be ready to lend a hand, be a friend, and offer encouragement to your neighbors as God leads you.

God, the neighbors I'd like to pray for today are...

Knowing How to Pray

*We don't know what God wants us to pray for,
nor how we should pray. But the Holy Spirit prays
for us with groanings that cannot be expressed in words.*
ROMANS 8:26 NLT

You find yourself facing a difficult situation, and you really aren't sure how to pray. Perhaps an elderly family member is dying or friends ask you to pray but don't give any details.

The Bible tells us that because we don't always know how to pray, the Holy Spirit prays for us in accordance with God's will. Our role in prayer, then, is to partner with the Holy Spirit in praying for the need.

So how do you do this? Begin by asking the Holy Spirit for wisdom. This is an important but easily overlooked step. The Holy Spirit knows exactly what to pray for all people in order to advance the purposes of God in their lives. Ask Him to guide you and then listen carefully with your spiritual ears. Pray whatever comes to your mind. Don't analyze it—just pray. Then trust the Holy Spirit to do His work. You can be certain He will!

God, some of the situations where I will need Your wisdom are...

Praying with Confidence

This is the secret: Christ lives in you. This gives you assurance of sharing his glory.
COLOSSIANS 1:27 NLT

Committing yourself to pray for someone—whether in person or from afar—can be intimidating. *Who am I to pray?* you might be thinking to yourself. *I'm nobody. I have so many flaws and I've made so many mistakes, why would God listen to me?*

Your flaws and mistakes don't define you in God's eyes. If you have invited Jesus into your life, He has annulled all the missteps in your past and made you worthy to come into God's presence. You have become God's child through the work of Jesus.

You can pray with confidence for yourself or others regardless of your past because your relationship with Jesus is not based on your good—or bad—behavior. If you've given the controls of your life to Jesus, then God sees you through Jesus-colored glasses.

Because Christ lives in you, you are invited to pray boldly. Nothing will prevent your Father in heaven from hearing you. Set aside all fear and insecurity and let God hear your voice.

Lord God, help me as I pray confidently for...

_____

_____

_____

_____

_____

_____

_____

December 2

To Be Used By God

God...will not forget your work and
the love you have shown him as you have helped
his people and continue to help them.
HEBREWS 6:10

God's readiness to use you in someone else's life is based more on your willingness than your worthiness. Perhaps you assume that God requires a long track record of good behavior in order for you to take part in His plans. On the contrary. God is looking for people who love Him and desire to be extensions of His love to others.

Men and women of God's choosing realize that He works most powerfully through people who depend wholly upon Him. They are willing to risk reputation, comfort, and security knowing that their God is bigger than any crisis or need. Even when they lack the skill or resources, they take comfort in knowing that with God, all things are possible.

If you're willing to be used by God, ask Him to show you who you can help. Don't be intimidated by your imperfections. He knows all there is to know and still He invites you to help. Take His hand and step out on behalf of someone in need.

Father God, knowing that You trust me makes me feel...

The People God Uses

Ask the Lord of the harvest, therefore, to send out workers into his harvest field.
LUKE 10:2

If you watch religious television, you might assume that God only uses impressive people who have dynamic personalities and are dripping with wisdom, intelligence, and Bible knowledge.

Jesus, however, wasn't impressed by "impressive" people.

Once, overwhelmed by the number of people in need, Jesus asked His heavenly Father to send *laborers* into His harvest field. Instead of asking for God to send educated, uniquely gifted people, He asked for common, everyday workers. Not pastors or priests. Rather, plumbers, house-wives, business people—men and women who look a lot like you. Not individuals who address thousands at a time, but people willing to pray for others and lend a helping hand—one person at a time.

While God uses uniquely gifted individuals, He also desires to use everyday people like you to change the world. If you feel called to pray for people in need, don't be put off because you don't think your abilities are impressive. When God calls on you to pray—just do it. Pleasing God is always impressive.

Lord God, I believe You want to use me through...

The Anointing of God

You have an anointing from the Holy One.
1 JOHN 2:20

When a new king was about to assume the throne in Bible times, a religious leader or prophet would *anoint* the incoming monarch with olive oil in a sacred ceremony. The oil, poured over his head, served as a visual and mystical symbol of God's blessing, authority, and power. Afterward, the king enjoyed the legal right to make decisions and act with the confidence that God was supporting him.

When you give your life to Jesus, you are anointed with the power of God. In other words, you are filled with God's blessing, authority, and power. You don't need to ask God to anoint you because He has already done it! You are already anointed by God to pray for others.

Pray for people, then, with confidence. Know that your prayers are going directly from your lips to God's ear. Ask God to open your eyes to the needs all around you. Through the Holy Spirit, He will lead you to those who need your prayers most. Let God use you to make a big difference in the lives of those around you.

Heavenly Father, I pray You will open my eyes so I can see...

Being Led in Prayer

All who are led by the Spirit of God are children of God.
ROMANS 8:14 NLT

"God lead me." Perhaps you've prayed that prayer when making a difficult decision or praying for a friend or loved one. But if you have given your life to Jesus, His Holy Spirit already lives in you. And because His Holy Spirit lives in you, God is already leading you as you pray.

The Bible tells us that the Holy Spirit intercedes for us in accordance with God's will. In other words, He's praying for you and through you when you pray. Deep inside, whether you feel His presence or not, the Holy Spirit is moving you to pray and telling you how to pray. He's filling you with compassion and directing your steps. Even when you feel like you've said the wrong thing, you can be confident that the Holy Spirit is already guiding your thoughts and your words. You may not understand His ways in the moment, but someday—perhaps in eternity—you will be able to see that the Holy Spirit was leading you the whole time.

Heavenly Father, I call on Your Holy Spirit to lead me as I pray for...

December 6

The Ministry of Intercession

I urge that supplications, prayers, intercessions,
and thanksgivings be made for all people.
1 TIMOTHY 2:1 ESV

Imagine what life would be like if we only prayed for ourselves. Our family and friends would never feel the encouragement that comes from other people praying for them. Instead, they would live day-by-day without the prayer support they desperately need. Consider the fact that for many people, this is already true. No one is praying for them. Not one.

For this reason, God calls His people to the ministry of intercession. To intercede means to speak on behalf of someone else. Intercessory prayer, then, means praying for someone, even when we don't know what to pray. It involves listening and praying. You're listening to the Holy Spirit who already lives inside you and who is already praying—and then voicing it to your Father in heaven.

To intercede for someone, begin by praying anything that comes to mind regarding that person. Then listen. What is the Holy Spirit praying inside you? Even if what comes to mind makes little sense, go ahead and pray about it. Then trust that through the Holy Spirit, you have made a difference for someone.

Lord God, I want to take part in intercessory prayer for...

_____

_____

_____

_____

_____

_____

_____

Finding Perspective in God's Presence

When I tried to understand all this, it troubled me deeply till I entered the sanctuary of God.
PSALM 73:16–17

He served as King David's chief choral director, responsible for leading Israel in singing praises to God. He also contributed at least a dozen entries to the book of Psalms. Asaph was respected by many as an insightful, creative, and godly man.

But something deeply bothered him: the success of the wicked. While many of his godly friends experienced hardship and grief, his ungodly friends skipped through life with hardly a worry or care, while amassing more and more wealth. Exasperated, he questioned whether he had served God in vain.

Have you ever felt like Asaph? Perhaps you diligently and faithfully serve God, yet you experience relentless hardship or grief. Then you see people who couldn't care less about God, and they're doing just fine. Left unresolved, this could undermine your faith.

The Bible tells us that Asaph resolved his dilemma by spending time in the life-giving presence of God. When you're disturbed by life's contradictions, spend time in His presence. Only there will you find true perspective.

Lord in Heaven, as I enter Your presence, I want to say...

As Natural as Breathing

Those who trust God's action in them find that
God's Spirit is in them—living and breathing God!
ROMANS 8:5 MSG

Breathing requires two activities: inhaling and exhaling. In order to inhale, we must first exhale. But in order to exhale, we must first inhale. Both are essential to life and without both, we would die.

In the same way, we all need God's life-giving Spirit to fill us. But just as we can't last very long holding our breath, we can't hold in the Spirit but must let Him flow out to others. Some people live as if they're holding their breath all day long. Others act as if they're constantly out of breath. God, on the other hand, desires to fill us and then use us.

Here's an exercise in prayer that will help you. As you inhale, say "Fill me." Then as you exhale, say "Use me." Repeat this again and again as you breathe.

Following this rhythm of prayer will create expectancy as you go about your day, an openness to step up when you become aware of a need. You will be spiritually healthy and ready to respond at all times.

Father God, Your Spirit within me makes me feel...

Knowing God

Let him who boasts boast of this,
that he understands and knows Me.
JEREMIAH 9:24 NASB

Over the centuries, thousands of books have been written about prayer. Some focus on praying correctly; others on persevering in prayer or employing prayer to fight evil—the choices are endless. For the most part, all of that is good—as long as one important piece isn't overlooked. Knowing God.

Prayer isn't a tool we use to get what we want from God. Prayer is the language we speak in order to know Him. Without aspiring to know and enjoy the God who created us, prayer exists as little more than a task.

Truly knowing someone is the fruit of quality *and* quantity time together. No shortcuts exist that will enable you to know Him quickly. You must spend time with Him. Fortunately, you can bring God with you wherever you go. In fact, He is already present wherever you're going. And that's the path that usually leads to knowing Him: Acknowledging Him wherever you are. Sharing life together. Laughing. Crying. Leaning on Him when you're weak. Eventually, you understand not only His ways, but His heart.

That's when your prayers become powerful.

Heavenly Father, some of the things I'm eager to know about You are...

Trusting God

Keep company with GOD, get in on the best.
Open up before GOD, keep nothing back;
he'll do whatever needs to be done.
PSALM 37:4–5 MSG

Prayer by its very definition involves giving up control to God. When you pray, you address someone you cannot see, often asking Him to do what you cannot do for yourself. That means you must trust the one you are praying to.

Have you ever prayed and then taken matters into your own hands? Maybe you accepted a lesser-paying job rather than wait for the one God was opening to you. Or you jumped into a relationship before receiving the peace that signals that person is God's choice. Those actions imply a lack of trust in God's wisdom and faithfulness.

As you grow in your relationship with God and get to know Him better, you realize that He loves you more than you love yourself. His faithfulness is far greater than yours, His power and wisdom deeper. You realize that you can trust Him, even when He says no or gives you no apparent answer at all. You trust Him because you know Him—regardless of your circumstances.

Heavenly Father, I have learned to trust You through...

Continue to Trust

He is a rewarder of those who diligently seek Him.
HEBREWS 11:6 NKJV

Giving up is easy. Actually, it requires nothing at all.

Quite often, crises drive us to our knees as we seek God's intervention. For many people, their most intimate moments with God occur in the midst of a crisis, when they realize their need for Jesus. But when our crisis becomes prolonged, we can easily lose our strength and resolve. Our disappointment with God's apparent inaction can turn into anger, which slowly mutates into bitterness. Eventually we give up seeking God altogether.

Diligently seeking God through a crisis—from start to finish—isn't for the fainthearted. It requires an enormous amount of faith in God's power and character. The reward comes to those who diligently seek Him. E. M. Bounds, the great champion of prayer, once wrote, "Faith is narrowed down to one particular thing—it does not believe that God will reward everybody, nor that He is a rewarder of all who pray, but that He is a rewarder of them who diligently seek Him." Will you continue to trust God until you get your answer?

Lord God, there are some situations where I gave up too easily, like...

Persevering in Prayer

Blessed is the one who perseveres under trial, because,
having stood the test, that person will receive the crown of life
that the Lord has promised to those who love him.
JAMES 1:12

Long-distance runners know that at some point in their race they will "hit the wall" as their bodies grow tired and begin breaking down. Weaknesses become exaggerated and every footfall is strained. Everything within them screams to give up, but they know they must push through if they want to finish the race and win the prize.

In the same way, we all face times when we hit the wall in prayer. Persevering without any visible change tests our will and strengthens our faith. Centuries ago, sages who knew God deeply referred to this as importunate prayer. "Importunate" means "persistent." They knew that answers are rarely won in the first ten minutes. Sometimes the answer we seek lies at the finish line, long after we hit the wall.

In order to win the prize, you must cling to God with a tenacious grip and trust that He will either answer your prayer or change it to conform to His will.

Father, I will persist in trusting You with...

Seeking God without a Crisis

Without faith it is impossible to please God.
HEBREWS 11:6

Almost everyone is up for praying during a crisis. The adrenaline is flowing, and other people are eager to add their voices to ours in order to see a dramatic outcome. But what happens when there is no crisis? How do we diligently seek God for the long haul? How do we stay tuned in when things seem to be rolling along smoothly?

While cultivating a daily discipline of prayer is important, without something more, our faith can easily grow as old, cold, and lifeless as a chilly December day. How do we keep our faith fresh? The Bible says that we are to *live* by faith. We are to take risks. Not foolish risks, obviously. But we are to live in a way that forces us to rely on God and diligently seek Him. It's the only kind of life that is pleasing to Him.

Avoid the safe options and explore opportunities that require you to venture outside of your comfort zone. Seek God diligently as you investigate the alternatives, then join Him in the adventure!

Heavenly Father, one adventure I would like to share with You is...

The Reward for Seeking God

Watch out that you do not lose what we have worked for,
but that you may be rewarded fully.
2 JOHN 1:8

For most people, the greatest motivator for prayer is human need. Whether big or small, our needs drive us to God. The Bible consistently reminds us that God rewards those who seek Him. He always rewards our diligent prayers—even though He doesn't always grant our requests, at least not in the way we expect. So what is the reward?

He is the reward.

When you diligently seek God, He gives you glimpses of His character. At one moment He may reveal His faithfulness, and at other moments His patience, wisdom, or peace. The facets of God's character are infinite. But without human need driving us, we would never know the vast depths of His love.

As you grow in intimacy with Him, however, you realize that you can trust Him. You can remain at peace when He says no because you understand that He is only interested in working good in your life. Seek Him in the good times and in times of need. The reward will make it well worth your while.

Father, some of the needs I bring to You are...

Where to Find Faith

No one can have faith without hearing the message about Christ.
ROMANS 10:17 CEV

If you were to compile a list of what pleases God most, faith would appear at the top. Faith is defined as trust and reliance on God. Living by faith is the opposite of living safe because faith always involves an element of risk. Without it, we cannot please God.

So how do you go about getting more faith? The Bible says that faith doesn't come from you, it comes from God. This places you in a precarious position because God wants something from you that you cannot manufacture on your own.

The Bible also says that faith comes from hearing the message about Christ. That message can be heard through sermons, Bible reading, fellowship with others who love God, and through meditative prayer. Your faith will grow as you prayerfully reflect on Him. His message is this: God loved us so much that he sent His Son to earth to save us from ourselves. When you give your life to Him, He promises to make His home in you. And if God can do anything, through Him, you can too!

Lord God, what I think it means to have faith is...

Why Forgive?

Bear with one another and, if anyone has a complaint against another,
forgive each other; just as the Lord has forgiven you, so you also must forgive.
COLOSSIANS 3:13 NRSV

"Forgive us our debts as we forgive our debtors."

Jesus' unsettling words from the Lord's Prayer can cause anyone to squirm. We all want to be forgiven, but forgiving others? Well, that's not so easy. But left unresolved, unforgiveness will always affect your relationship with God because it minimizes the price Jesus paid for your offenses. It's saying you aren't so bad so it was no big deal for God to forgive you, but the person who has sinned against you is another story.

If you feel a sense of distance between you and God, examine your heart for any trace of unforgiveness. Some wounds are so deep that forgiveness takes time. God understands that. He just wants you to take that first step on the path to forgiveness.

Forgiveness doesn't mean the offense committed against you was unimportant or insignificant. It means you're willing to pardon the person who wronged you because *you* have been pardoned.

Lord God, I feel I need to forgive...

....

....

....

....

....

....

....

Praying for Your Enemies

Love your enemies and pray for those who persecute you,
that you may be children of your Father in heaven.
MATTHEW 5:44–45

Praying for your family and friends? Easy. Praying for people who use and abuse you? Hard. Really hard.

Praying for the people who hurt you may seem like cruel and unusual punishment. And yet Jesus commands us to pray for the people who abuse us. But don't think that Jesus wasn't willing to back up His words. When He hung on the cross, Jesus prayed for *His* abusers saying, "Father, forgive them, for they know not what they do."

Praying for someone will change your perspective about that person. As you pray, the one you are praying for becomes more human. Your sense of compassion grows stronger. And even more importantly, you begin to see the person from God's perspective. Over time, the offense fades as you realize God loves that person as much as He loves you. In the end, you are both freed to live more abundant lives.

Father God, I believe You are asking me to pray for...

....

....

....

....

....

....

....

Waiting for the Answer

I wait for the LORD, my soul does wait, and in His word do I hope.
PSALM 130:5 NASB

By the time Mary gave birth to Jesus, the entire universe was pregnant with anticipation. For more than a thousand years, the prophets foretold the coming of the Messiah. That's right—*a thousand years,* and yet He had not appeared.

How long are you willing to wait for God to answer your prayer? A week? A month? A lifetime? Doesn't your wait seem just a little inconsequential compared to that of so many who prayed for the Messiah to come throughout their lifetimes and yet never lived to see Him?

Few people like to wait. Yet waiting for your prayers to be answered is not a waste of time. Waiting gives you an opportunity to examine your motivations and evaluate whether your request is self-focused or God-focused. And it requires you to lean more and more on God.

The Messiah did arrive right on time and brought joy to the world. Your answer will also come in God's perfect time. He will not fail you.

Father, some of the things I'm learning as I wait include...

Highly Favored

The angel went to her and said, "Greetings, you who are highly favored! The Lord is with you."
LUKE 1:28

Imagine Mary's consternation when the angel of the Lord appeared, telling her she was highly favored and that God was with her. Beginning an announcement that way can only mean one thing: This isn't going to be easy. But imagine being told that you are going to give birth to the Messiah—and you are going to conceive the baby without the involvement of a man. Who would believe such a story? Mary's mysterious pregnancy would jeopardize her relationship with her fiancé, Joseph, and leave her to live down the notion that she was a loose woman. Nevertheless, Mary believed the angel's words.

Perhaps you feel overwhelmed right now and your life seems to be in chaos. That doesn't mean God is absent or punishing you. You can be in the middle of trouble and in the middle of God's favor at the same time.

Let your prayer of commitment be like Mary's: "I am Your servant. Let it be just as You have said."

Dear Lord, I believe You are in the middle of my trouble because...

Mary's Words

Mary said, "Here am I, the servant of the Lord; let it be with me according to your word."
LUKE 1:38 NRSV

When the angel appeared to Mary telling her that she was about to conceive an illegitimate son—in a culture that frowned on such behavior—she was initially troubled. She understood that if the angel's words came true, it would significantly impact the rest of her life. But after further explanation, she replied, "May it be to me as you have said." Mary, who was likely between fourteen and sixteen years old at the time, displayed maturity and trust in God well beyond her years.

To what extent can you say to God, "May it be to me as You have said"? When life follows our plans, we can recite Mary's words without a problem. But when we're faced with situations we hadn't anticipated—like a newborn son with Down syndrome or the death of a spouse—the words don't flow so easily.

Whatever it is you are facing, listen prayerfully to what God is saying to you about the situation, and then trust Him—like Mary did.

Lord God, Mary's words give me courage as I face...

Hope in Human Form

No one who hopes in you will ever be put to shame.
PSALM 25:3

To the cancer patient, chemotherapy represents the hope of a healthier future. To the unemployed, additional education represents the hope of financial stability. To a couple in marital distress, counseling represents the hope of a better relationship. We all need hope. Without it, we wither and die, or just give up.

For more than a thousand years, the people of Israel waited expectantly for the Messiah to appear. On Him they set their hopes for freedom and the establishment of God's kingdom on earth.

Then, on that holy night, hope was born in a manger. His name was Jesus. "The hopes and fears of all the years are met in thee tonight," the line from Joseph Mohr's *Silent Night, Holy Night* declares. In Him, you can place all of your hopes because He is hope in human form. The Bible describes Him as Wonderful Counselor, Mighty God, Everlasting Father, and Prince of Peace. Bring your prayers to Him; hope in Him.

Wonderful Father, I put my hope in ...

The God of Surprises

There were shepherds out in the field,
keeping watch over their flock by night.
And an angel of the Lord appeared to them.
LUKE 2:8–9 ESV

They were just doing their jobs. Night after night, day after day, this particular group of shepherds was charged with protecting their flocks of sheep, many of which likely ended up as sacrifices on the temple altar to the God of Israel. Because their job required constant oversight, they were unavailable to worship alongside their Jewish brothers and sisters. As a result, they were treated as spiritual undesirables in their society. Not exactly the kind of men who would claim that angels appeared to them.

But one dark night an angel from heaven did indeed appear to the shepherds, announcing the birth of Jesus. Think about it: The first people the angels told about the birth of Jesus were arguably the most unspiritual in their society.

And God continues the practice today. In His love and mercy, God reveals Himself to even the most unspiritual people. He speaks to us when we aren't listening for Him or looking for Him. Prayer is a conversation. Are you listening for His voice?

Lord God, I believe You are saying...

God in the Details

Mary treasured all these words and pondered them in her heart.
LUKE 2:19 NRSV

She was forced to travel eighty miles, an eight-day journey from Nazareth to Bethlehem by donkey, while practically full term. Then, when she arrived at her destination, Mary and her husband, Joseph, couldn't even find a room in which to give birth to the Messiah.

After thousands of years of prophecies and preparation, you'd think God would at least provide something better than a dirty stable to house the birth of His only Son. Yet into the chaos of this world, the Son of God was born. Cows mooing.

Minimal privacy. Germs crawling everywhere.

Sometimes even though we pray, things seem to go haywire. Worst-case scenarios come to pass. But be assured that the God who entered the reality of our human existence is concerned about your request. While orchestrating world events, He also oversees the details of your life, even when they seem chaotic. You might feel awkward, confused, even overwhelmed—but be encouraged. Mary and Joseph dealt with similar struggles. And look how that turned out.

Heavenly Father, thank You for bringing Your glory to my level. Encourage me to...

He Really Understands

The Word became flesh and lived among us,
and we have seen his glory, the glory as
of a father's only son, full of grace and truth.
JOHN 1:14 NRSV

When God sent His only son Jesus into the world, He chose a woman named Mary to give Jesus life, clothing Him with human skin. Jesus didn't suddenly appear as a mysterious emanation proclaiming that God understands and cares. Rather, Jesus became a human being, a vulnerable baby born to a poor peasant couple in a dusty stable and placed in a dirty manger.

In the midst of our daily lives, we can easily assume that God simply doesn't understand us. He can't understand our futile efforts to rescue an overdrawn bank account or the overwhelming grief of losing a loved one. He doesn't feel the frustration of a wayward child.

Yet God *does* understand. He has shown mercy to generations of wayward children. He knows the grief of losing an only son. In the same way, Jesus *does* understand poverty and the pain of loss and separation.

When you cry out to Him in prayer, know that He intimately and completely understands.

Dear Father, thank You for understanding how I feel about...

The Power of Paradox

An angel of the Lord appeared to Joseph in a dream.
"Get up! Flee to Egypt with the child and his mother," the angel said.
"Stay there until I tell you to return, because Herod is going
to search for the child to kill him."
MATTHEW 2:13 NLT

Few people feel at peace living with paradox—a phrase or action that seemingly contradicts itself. We want our lives to make sense according to our understanding. Saying prayers to God and believing Him to be good in the midst of our pain is a paradox that causes many to stumble. How can God allow pain and evil in the world and still be good?

And yet the Christmas story is full of paradoxes: God becoming a human being. The King of the universe lying in a manger. The royal magi presenting a peasant child with gifts of gold, frankincense, and myrrh. A king intent on murdering an infant.

Nothing God does is contradictory. Which brings us back to the baby in the manger. What didn't make sense in that moment became the salvation of the whole world. God knew what He was doing then—and He knows what He's doing now. He can be trusted with your prayers.

Holy God, I trust You with my prayers about...

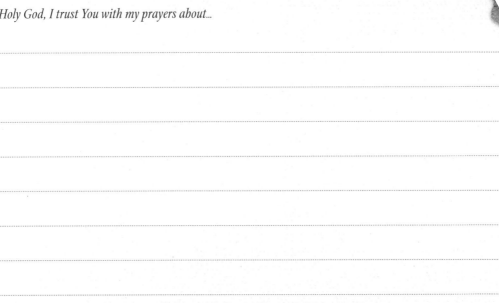

God's Heart

I will praise you, Lord my God, with all my heart; I will glorify your name forever.
PSALM 86:12

The Bible tells us that when our prayers align with God's will, great things happen. Sure, God could accomplish His will by Himself (He often does), but He prefers to work through us and our prayers.

Setting aside our personal requests for a moment, what are the issues on God's heart? They involve anything that brings more glory to Him. On the one hand, God's glory—the evidence of His goodness and love—is present all around us. The problem is that we usually overlook it. Nature is an obvious example. Think of a breathtaking sunset or trees bowing under a fresh blanket of sparkling snow.

Yet God reveals His glory in other ways: a hardened heart that softens toward Him through pain. A scientist who credits Him for helping her create a new vaccine. Look at your life: How can God be glorified in you and in the lives of the people around you? Pray for what is on God's heart and let His glory flow through you.

Lord God, I pray that You would glorify Yourself through me by...

Kingdom Prayer

*The kingdom of God is not a matter of eating
and drinking but of righteousness,
peace and joy in the Holy Spirit.*
ROMANS 14:17

Jesus taught that through Him, God's kingdom was present and future. Theologians define the kingdom of God as God's rule and reign. For example, a British subject remains a subject of the king or queen of England regardless of what country he or she is in. In the same way, the kingdom isn't determined by location as much as the rule and reign of God in a person's heart. So the kingdom of God is present through people submitted to Him, yet the full and unhindered reign of the kingdom has not yet occurred.

That's where your prayers make a difference.

Jesus taught us to pray, "Thy kingdom come, Thy will be done." God's deepest desire for this world is for its inhabitants to yield to His rule and reign. Not so He can dominate us like a tyrannical dictator, but because it is only through Him that we will experience true life—in this life and the life to come.

Will you pray that we all will yield to God's life-giving rule and reign?

Father, I yield to Your rule and reign. My prayers for Your kingdom are...

....

....

....

....

....

....

Prayerful Selah

Who is this King of glory? The LORD of hosts, He is the King of glory. Selah.
PSALM 24:10 NKJV

Both Thanksgiving and Christmas have passed, and in only four days, people around the world will be celebrating the new year. For many, New Year's Day serves as a boundary line between the past and the future. The new year represents a new beginning—and the opportunity to purge ourselves of elements in our past that we'd prefer to forget. Taking time for prayerful reflection can help you identify what needs to be cleansed, improved, or discarded.

In ancient Israel, opportunities for prayerful reflection were woven into the people's worship practices. Throughout the Old Testament book of Psalms, the Hebrew word *selah* appears. The word was used in ancient Hebrew songs to introduce a musical interlude and call people to reflect on the words in the song.

Your life is a song, and soon you're going to transition to the next verse. Why not take a little time right now for a *selah*—a prayerful reflection to assess the last year?

Heavenly Father, as I prayerfully reflect, my thoughts are...

Clean and Forgiven

With the heart one believes unto righteousness,
and with the mouth confession is made unto salvation.
ROMANS 10:10 NKJV

Louis Cassels, former United Press International religion editor, once wrote, "In confession...we open our lives to healing, reconciling, restoring, uplifting grace of Him who loves us in spite of what we are." Confession exposes our rebellion, shame, and brokenness to God's healing, reconciling, and restoring light. The Bible tells us that when we confess our faults to God He promises to forgive and cleanse us of anything that stands between us and Him.

Preparing for the new year affords all of us the opportunity to make confession to God.

That way, we can enter the new year clean—like taking a spiritual shower.

Your Father in heaven longs to be completely restored to you. So boldly profess your faults—not only those things you've done but also those things you've said or thought. Reflect on the things you should have done but neglected doing, and confess them. Avoid defending or explaining yourself—just voice them to God. Then allow the shower of God's forgiveness to make you fully clean.

Loving heavenly Father, I confess to You...

The Power of Consecration

Consecrate yourselves and be holy, because I am the LORD your God.
LEVITICUS 20:7

The word for "consecrate" appears almost two hundred times in the Old Testament. It can be translated to mean "holy," "dedicated," or "appointed." But the word can be translated most clearly to mean "set apart." Consecrating yourself to God means to set yourself apart for God, not only in terms of His will, but also setting yourself apart to know Him and include Him in every aspect of your life.

In two days, you will begin a new year. It's a chance to renew your intentions to fully consecrate yourself to Him: your plans, your relationships, your job, your finances, your time, your thoughts, your prayers. It is the perfect time to fully set all of these things apart from the rest of the world. Ask yourself, *What would my life look like if I was fully consecrated to God?*

Then aim to be that person.

Heavenly Father, in the coming year, I give You...

Dreaming God's Dreams

Call to me and I will answer you, and will tell you great and hidden things that you have not known.
JEREMIAH 33:3 NRSV

"I have a dream," Martin Luther King Jr. famously spoke on the steps of the Lincoln Memorial in 1963. He dreamed of a day when his fellow Americans would recognize that all people are created equal. The esteemed orator wasn't necessarily referring to the kind of dream that awakens our imaginations in the middle of the night. He was talking about a preferred reality that lies in our future; a possibility that resides beyond our grasp if we choose to do what we've always done.

God wants you to dream *His* dreams. He invites you to join Him in making a difference. Be aware, though, that dreaming God's dreams might not bring you wealth and a long life. Jesus lived a life of poverty and dreamed of reconciling humankind with their God. Attaining it cost Him His life. The same applied to Dr. King. Dreaming God's dreams, though, enables you to partner with God in prayer and change your world. Forever.

Father God, the prayer You have placed in my heart to pray for the world is...

Ellie Claire® Gift & Paper Expressions
Brentwood, TN 37027
EllieClaire.com

Come Away with Me: A 365-Day Devotional Journal
© 2014 by Ellie Claire
Ellie Claire is a registered trademark of Worthy Media, Inc.

ISBN 978-1-60936-957-6

Stock or custom editions of Ellie Claire titles may be purchased in bulk for educational, business, ministry, fundraising, or sales promotional use. For information, please e-mail info@EllieClaire.com

Devotional writing by Dwight Clough, Adam Colwell, and Michael Klassen in association with Snapdragon Group, Tulsa, OK.

Cover and interior design by Jeff Jansen | AestheticSoup.net

Printed in China

3 4 5 6 7 8 9 – 19 18 17 16 15